INTERPRETING
THE
SYMBOLS
AND
TYPES

KEVIN J. CONNER

CITYBIBLE
PUBLISHING

www.citybiblepublishing.com

INTERPRETING THE SYMBOLS AND TYPES

COMPLETELY REVISED AND EXPANDED

KEVIN J. CONNER

Published by City Bible Publishing
9200 NE Fremont
Portland, Oregon 97220

Printed in U.S.A.

City Bible Publishing is a ministry of City Bible Church and is dedicated to serving the local church and its leaders through the production and distribution of quality materials.

It is our prayer that these materials, proven in the context of the local church, will equip leaders in exalting the Lord and extending His kingdom.

For a free catalog of additional resources from City Bible Publishing please call 1-800-777-6057 or visit our web site at www.citybiblepublishing.com.

Foreword

The Christian culture, like any other culture, has a language all of its own. It is the language of Divine origin - the language of the sign and symbol, in the use of which the Bible abounds.

Many times believers, both young and old, hear preachers and teachers use symbolic expressions in the course of their sermons or expositions. Often the language becomes unintelligible because the hearer does not understand or is unable to interpret, the symbol or type used. It is with a desire to help believers understand "the language of the symbol and type" that this book is written.

Symbolology and typology are the most neglected fields of study. Types and symbols are regarded by many as of little importance. However, much of the richness of Scripture truth is lost if the believer does not acquaint himself with the language of the symbol and type.

God has woven throughout His Books numerous symbols and types, each revealing characteristics and shades of meaning that would be lost to the bible student were such not there. One cannot understand much of the language of the Bible without understanding of the symbol and the language of the type.

Many expositors who fear lapsing into allegorization of Scripture avoid this area of interpretation.

However, it should be borne in mind that, when the true Biblical meaning or interpretation of a symbol or type is based solidly on the actual meaning of the words, no one need fear allegorization. Once the interpretation of the symbols and types is discovered, the meaning is consistent throughout the total Word. It does not change. There is but *one interpretation*, but there may be *many applications*.

The format of the book falls into two sections. The first section deals with the Symbolical Principle, while the latter section deals with the Typical Principle of interpreting the Scriptures. Woven through both of these are the Numerical Principle and Christo-centric Principle of interpreting the Word. The student is referred to the Bibliography.

The text here is by no means exhaustive. To deal fully with each symbol and type would require a large volume. Enough has been given in "seed" for the earnest and wise student to develop within the framework of Biblical hermeneutics.

To obtain the greatest benefit from the book, the reader is encouraged to:

1. Consider the Scripture references given to interpret the symbol and type. The Scripture MUST be read, as the references are too numerous to have been quoted here.

2. Make a brief comparison of the common characteristics between the symbol/type and that which is symbolized/typified.

3. Extend his study, if desired, by searching out, in Strong's Exhaustive Concordance (or other Concordances), the other uses of the word in Scripture.

"It is the glory of God to conceal a thing, but it is the honor of kings to search out a matter" (Pr 25:2).

Acknowledgment

Special thanks must go to brother Dick Andrew for his part in the production of the original edition and the many thousands of books produced from that edition. Numerous hours were spent in editing, proofing and checking Scriptures as well as acting in an advisory capacity as to the arrangement of the book. His suggestions and voluntary help were greatly appreciated.

The author of this updated text would also like to acknowledge the work of Carl C. Harwood, Handbook of Bible Types and Symbols, a booklet that apparently is no longer in print.

In Chapter Eighteen, "Alphabetical Listing of Symbols and Types," the author has drawn heavily from this little work, along with further additions, Scriptures and update, according to this present format.
In this edition, the total text has been updated and additional material, Scriptures, and clarification have been provided.

The author trusts that this edition will be as great a blessing to students of the Word as was the original edition.

Kevin J. Conner

Recommendations

Recommendations are made here to the student on how best to use this present textbook.

As the student looks up the reference for any symbol and/or type in Chapter 1-17, according to their respective classifications, then, for fuller comments and additional Scriptures, the student should then turn to the listing of that same symbol or type in its Alphabetical Listing, Chapter 18.

Index To Abbreviations of Bible Books

OLD TESTAMENT

Genesis	Ge
Exodus	Ex
Leviticus	Lev
Numbers	Nu
Deuteronomy	Dt
Joshua	Jos
Judges	Jdg
Ruth	Ru
1 Samuel	1Sa
2 Samuel	2Sa
1 Kings	1Ki
2 Kings	2Ki
1 Chronicles	1Ch
2 Chronicles	2Ch
Ezra	Ezr
Nehemiah	Ne
Esther	Est
Job	Job
Psalm(s)	Ps(s)
Proverbs	Pr
Ecclesiastes	Ecc
Song of Songs	SS
Isaiah	Isa
Jeremiah	Jer
Lamentations	La
Ezekiel	Eze
Daniel	Da
Hosea	Hos
Joel	Joel
Amos	Am
Obadiah	Ob
Jonah	Jnh
Micah	Mic
Nahum	Na
Habakkuk	Hab
Zephaniah	Zep
Haggai	Hag
Zechariah	Zec
Malachi	Mal

NEW TESTAMENT

Matthew	Mt
Mark	Mk
Luke	Lk
John	Jn
Acts	Ac
Romans	Ro
1 Corinthians	1Co
2 Corinthians	2Co
Galatians	Gal
Ephesians	Eph
Philippians	Php
Colossians	Col
1 Thessalonians	1Th
2 Thessalonians	2Th
1 Timothy	1Ti
2 Timothy	2Ti
Titus	Tit
Philemon	Phm
Hebrews	Heb
James	Jas
1 Peter	1Pe
2 Peter	2Pe
1 John	1Jn
2 John	2Jn
3 John	3Jn
Jude	Jude
Revelation	Rev

TABLE OF CONTENTS

SECTION ONE

The Symbolic Principle

It is impossible to properly and fully interpret the symbols in Scripture without a proper understanding of the language of the symbol.

The Bible is written in the language of the symbol as well as the language of the type. In this section we begin with the interpretative principle, "The Symbolic Principle," and its guidelines before moving into the various categories of Biblical Symbols.

CHAPTER ONE

THE LANGUAGE OF THE SYMBOL

I.   THE LANGUAGE OF CREATION AND REDEMPTION

    A.   Genesis Chapters 1-2

The first several chapters of Genesis contain for us the record of creation. God gives but the briefest details of the creation of things pertaining to the natural and material realm. The creation of heaven and earth, waters and oceans, seed and herbs, fruit trees yielding fruit, sun, moon and stars, fish and fowl, beasts and man are covered in a few Scriptures. That is, a little over two chapters. The remainder of Scripture contains God's plan of redemption since the fall of man in Genesis chapter 3.

    B.   Genesis 1 - Revelation 22

The remainder of Scripture takes up the natural, the material or the created things and uses such to be symbolical of things pertaining to redemption. The whole of the Bible, from Genesis chapter 1 to Revelation chapter 22 abounds with such symbolism.

    C.   Job

It is for this reason that Job speaks: "But ask now the beasts, and they shall teach thee; and the fowls of the air, and they shall tell thee: or speak to the earth, and it shall teach thee: and the fishes of the sea shall declare unto thee. Who knoweth not in all these that the hand of the Lord hath wrought this?" (Job 12:7-9).

D.   David

And again, the Psalmist David says, "The heavens declare the glory of God, and the firmament sheweth His handywork. Day unto day uttereth speech, and night unto night sheweth knowledge. There is no speech nor language where their voice is not heard." (Ps 19:1-3 with Ro 10:17-18).

E.   Paul

the apostle Paul tells us: "For the invisible things of Him from the creation of the world are clearly seen, being understood by the things that are made, even His eternal power and Godhead; so that they are without excuse." (Ro 1:20).

Paul also lays down a principle of God when he says first the natural, then afterwards that which is spiritual (1Co 15:46).

Thus the Creator is telling man to look at His creations, for He is speaking a language to us by created things. Within the created things and creatures, God has hidden truth. For He takes "the language of creation" and it becomes "the language of the symbol" which in turn becomes "the language of redemption."

F.   Jesus

Jesus especially used symbolic language. It was God's secret code for veiling or revealing truth according to the attitude of the listener. He did this when He taught by the parabolic method. This is specially seen in Matthew 13 in the teaching on the Parables of the Kingdom. He spoke of the sower and the seed, wheat and tares, stony, thorny and good ground, birds, trees, fish, pearls and seas, etc.

G.　Disciples

> The multitude in general heard only "the language of creation", but the disciples realized it was "the language of the symbol" or "the language of redemption." They perceived by the interpretation of the parables that there was more to it than the natural, the literal and the material.

H.　Solomon

> As Solomon said in Pr 25:2: "It is the glory of God to conceal a thing, but the honor of kings to search out a matter."

Thus God has concealed truth in the symbolic use of created things. It is the honor of believers, as kings and priests unto God, to search these truths out.

II.　THE SYMBOLIC PRINCIPLE

> One of the important principles of hermeneutics (principles of interpreting the Scriptures) is the Symbolic Principle, the definition of which is as follows:

A.　Definition

> It is that principle by which the interpretation of a verse or passage of Scripture containing symbolic elements can be determined only by a proper interpretation of the symbol(s) involved.

B.　Amplification

> According to Webster's Dictionary, the word "symbol" is made up of two Greek words: "syn" meaning "together", and "ballein" meaning "to throw". It means literally "thrown together", and denotes an object used to represent something abstract: an emblem: using one thing to stand for or represent another.

Though the word "symbol" is not specifically used in the Bible, God caused the writers of Scripture to imply the literary method of symbolization throughout Scripture. They often used one thing to represent another because of common characteristics. This is what is meant by symbolization in which the link between that which is used as a symbol and that which is being symbolized is the characteristics common to both.

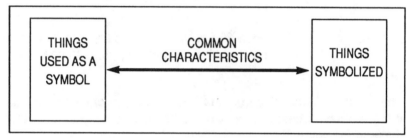

God, in authoring the Bible, dealt with both creation and redemption. The first two chapters of Genesis contain the record of the creation of the natural realm; the rest of the Bible contains God's plan of redemption. In Scripture, God uses the natural things He created to become symbols (Ro 1:19,20). In other words, as already mentioned, the language of creation becomes the language of the symbol which in turn becomes the language of redemption.

C.   Illustration

One of the major uses of the material realm used to symbolize and typify spiritual truth is that which pertained to the Tabernacle of Moses and then the Temple of Solomon. God instructed Moses to take things from the various created kingdoms to set forth symbolic truth.

From the mineral kingdom, the vegetable kingdom, the animal kingdom, and the human kingdom, God chose things and used them to symbolize truth in His spiritual kingdom (Ex 25:1-9; 35:1-29; 1Ch 28-29).

1. Mineral Kingdom

    Gold, silver and brass; precious stones, onyx stones for the ephod and for the breastplate - these were used to symbolize truth.

2. Vegetable Kingdom

    Fine linen, shittim (acacia) wood, olive oil for the light, spices for the anointing oil, and for the sweet incense -- these were used for symbolizing truth.

3. Animal Kingdom

    Cloths and dyes (crushed) from shellfish, of blue, purple and scarlet; goats' hair, rams' skins dyed red, badgers' skins, sheep, goats, oxen and birds for sacrifice -- all were used to symbolize Divine truths.

4. Human Kingdom

    Israelitish men and women were used by God in the offerings for the building of the Tabernacle of the Lord and the Temple of God, as well as for the Divine offices of priesthood and kingship.

5. Spiritual Kingdom

    The very fact that GOD HIMSELF specified the materials for both Tabernacle and Temple out of these kingdoms showed that there was some spiritual truth to be discovered, hidden in the external and material form (Ro 2:20). God is Spirit, yet He uses the material to symbolize or typify the spiritual (Jn 4:20-24, e.g., the natural well of water pointed to the spiritual well of water).

Therefore, if one is to understand the truths of the Tabernacle or Temple, which are hidden in the symbol, he must properly interpret the significance of the symbol!

Read also Heb 10:1; 8:4-5; Col 2:16-17.

III.   CLASSIFICATION OF SYMBOLS

Basically, there are eight categories of symbols in Scripture: (1) Objects, (2) Creatures, (3) Actions, (4) Numbers, (5) Names, (6) Colors, (7) Directions and (8) Places.

A.   Symbolic Objects

In Scripture, God used inanimate objects, whether God-created or man-made, as symbols.

Hos 7:8	"Ephraim is a <u>cake</u> not turned."
Ps 18:2	"The Lord is my <u>Rock</u>..."
Pr 18:2	"The Name of the Lord is a strong <u>tower</u>..."
Dt 32:2	"My doctrine shall drop as the <u>rain</u>..."
Ps 119:105	"Thy word is a <u>lamp</u> unto my feet..."
Rev 1:20	"The seven <u>stars</u> are the seven angels...the seven <u>candlesticks</u> are...the seven churches..."

B.   Symbolic Creatures

In Scripture God used living creatures, whether plants or animals, as symbols.

Da 7:17	"These great <u>beasts</u>... are four kings..."
Hos 7:11	"Ephraim also is like a silly <u>dove</u>..."
Lk 13:31,32	"Herod... that <u>fox</u>..."

Isa 40:31	"They that wait on the Lord... as <u>eagles</u>..."
Lk 8:11	"The <u>seed</u> is the Word of God..."
1Pe 1:24	"All flesh is as <u>grass</u> and all the glory of man as the <u>flower</u> of the grass..."
Jn 1:29,36	"Behold, Jesus... the <u>lamb</u> of God..."

C.   Symbolic Actions

In Scripture God used actions to be symbolic.

Ps 141:1,2	"...the <u>lifting</u> up of my hands as the evening sacrifice"
Ge 25:23-26	"Elder shall serve the younger...his hand <u>took hold</u> of Esau's heel..."
Jos 1:3	"Every place that the sole of your feet shall <u>tread</u> upon, that have I given you..."
Isa 31:1	"Woe to them that <u>go down</u> to Egypt for help...they look not to the Holy One of Israel..."

D.   Symbolic Numbers

In Scripture God attributed symbolic significance to numbers.

2Co 13:1	"this is the <u>third</u> time I am coming to you. In the mouth of two or three witnesses shall it be established.
Rev 13:18	"The number of a man; and his number is <u>six hundred threescore and six</u>..."
Mt 19:28	"...ye also shall sit upon

| | twelve thrones, judging the tribes of Israel..." |
| Ge 14:4 | "...in the thirteenth year they rebelled..." |

Note: Refer to "The Numerical Principle" under "Symbolic Numbers".

E. Symbolic Names

In Scripture God used names to be symbolic both personally and nationally. In Scripture a name is generally significant of the nature, character, experience, or function of the person, place or nation.

1Sa 25:25	"...for as his name is, so is he; Nabal (Fool) is his name, and folly is with him."
1Sa 4:21	"And she named the child Ichabod, saying the glory is departed from Israel."
Hos 1:9	"Then said God, Call his name Loammi: for ye are not My people and I will not be your God."
Mt 1:21	"Thou shalt call his name Jesus: for He shall save His people from their sins."
Jn 1:42	"Thou shall be called Cephas, which is by interpretation A Stone."

F. Symbolic Colors

In Scripture God attributed symbolic significance to colors.

Isa 1:18	"Though your sins be as scarlet, they shall be white as snow; though they be red like crimson, they shall be as wool."
Mk 15:17,18	"Jesus clothed in a purple garment...King of the Jews."
Rev 3:4,5	"They shall walk with Me in white for they are worthy..."
Rev 19:8	"The fine linen, clean and white ... righteousness of saints."

G.   Symbolic Directions

In Scripture God attributed symbolic significance to directions.

Jer 1:14	"Out of the north cometh forth evil..."
Eze 43:1,2	"toward the east, and behold the glory of the God of Israel came..."
2Ch 4:4	The 12 oxen under the molten sea, looked toward the north, south, east and west.
Da 8:4	The ram pushing westward, northward and southward...

H.   Symbolic Places

In Scripture God attributed symbolic significance to places, either specified or implied.

Ge 11:1-9	"Therefore the name of it is called Babel, because the Lord did there confound the language of all the earth." Babylon means "Confusion" (Rev 18)

11

| Heb 7:1-2 | "Melchizedek, king of Salem...King of righteousness, and after that, king of peace (Rev 21:2). |
| Ps 48:2 | "Beautiful for situation...is Mount Zion on the sides of the north." Zion means "elevation", pointing to heavenly Zion (Heb 12:22-24). |

It can be seen from the above illustrations that God, in authoring Scripture, utilized the literary method of symbolism. It is essential to recognize that since God is the virtual author of Scripture, He was able to cause symbols to carry the same significance consistently throughout the Bible.

It is the literary method of symbolism used in writing Scripture that gives rise to the Symbolic Principle of interpreting Scripture.

IV.   GUIDELINES FOR INTERPRETING SYMBOLS

In interpreting symbols, there need to be proper guidelines, as follows:

A.   The first step in using the Symbolic Principle is to rightly determine which elements of the verse under consideration are meant to be interpreted as symbols.

1.   If the language of the verse makes no literal or actual sense, then it must be interpreted as having symbolic sense (e.g., Rev 12:1-4; 13:1-2 with Da 7:1-4). The trite saying is true: "If the sense of Scripture makes common sense, then seek no other sense or you may fall into non-sense."

2.   If it does make literal or actual sense, then it can only be interpreted as having symbolic

sense when the Scripture interprets or intimates this to be the case in other verses (e.g., The Tabernacle, Jn 1:14; e.g., The Temple, 1Co 3:17).

B.   The interpreter must recognize the three fundamental elements of symbolism:

1.   The significance of a symbol is based upon the literal or actual nature and characteristics of that which is being used as a symbol.

2.   A symbol is meant to represent something essentially different from itself.

3.   The link between that which is used as a symbol and that which is symbolized is the characteristics common to both.

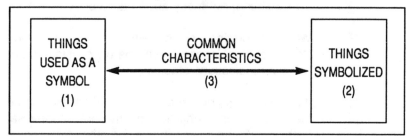

C.   The Symbolic Principle of interpretation must be used in conjunction with the Context Principle; that is, the whole context of Scripture. Because many symbols are used more than once in Scripture, it is proper to compare every usage of them to gain a complete understanding of the progressive unfolding of their symbolic significance.

D.   Generally speaking, the Bible interprets its own symbols. Thus, the interpreter must search through Scripture for the interpretation of the symbol under consideration.

E.   A study of the usages of the symbol in Scripture must be based on a consideration of the original languages (e.g., there are several different Hebrew words for "lion", each having its own significance).

F.   The interpreter must keep in mind that something may be used to symbolize more than one thing in Scripture. The same symbol may represent different characteristic aspects (e.g., Gold - used to represent Divine nature, God, wisdom, faith, etc.). Also, some symbols may have good and evil aspects to them (e.g., the lion used as a symbol of Jesus, His saints, and the Devil also - Rev 5:5; 1Pe 5:8, etc.). Symbols often have negative and positive or good and bad applications. (e.g., Birds, such as the dove or raven, symbolize spirits; the dove is symbolic of the Holy Spirit, and the raven symbolic of the evil spirit, yet both are birds.) Remember, there is but one interpretation, but many applications of symbols!

G.   When interpreting a symbol within a verse, its general Scriptural significance should be used unless there are clear indications otherwise.

H.   If the symbol is uninterpreted in the Word, investigate the context thoroughly for the thought or idea set forth; check the concordance for other references, and consider the nature of the symbol used as it may give the clue (e.g., Lion, swine, lamb, etc.). The nature of such will give the idea, whether it is specified or implied.

Note: It is worth remembering that Satan is the great counterfeiter of all that God does. He is not an originator, but a counterfeiter. God is the originator of all things, while Satan counterfeits all that God does.

Hence, the Bible does not condemn Astronomy, but Satan's counterfeit is Astrology and the worship of the heavenly bodies and constellations.

The Bible has much significance in the use of numbers, but Satan's counterfeit is Numerology where people seek to guide their lives by such.

The same is true of Bible symbols. Satan and the world of the occult have taken many of God's symbols and used them for counterfeit religious symbols (e.g., The Rainbow Cult, Numerology, Astrology, etc.).

The true believer is not to let the counterfeit rob him of the reality. The believer is not to let the error of cultic symbolism rob him of the truth of Divine symbolism. The Bible provides safe guidelines for principles of interpretation of these symbols which the believer should follow. This will prevent the student from falling into any counterfeit symbolism or allegorization of the Scriptures.

The author of this text has endeavored to follow these principles in listing the interpretation of both symbols and types as in the sacred Scriptures.

CHAPTER TWO

SYMBOLIC OBJECTS

In this chapter we come to the various groupings of Symbolic Objects and list them in alphabetical order.

The symbolic objects seen in this chapter find their categories under (A) Human, (B) Man-made, (C) Mineral, (D) Sky, (E) Supernatural and (F) Vegetable objects.

The briefest interpretation is given and Scripture which support the same also, whether specific or implied.

I.   SYMBOLIC OBJECTS - HUMAN

SYMBOL	INTERPRETATION	SCRIPTURES
Body	Dwelling place of the human spirit; tabernacle, temple of God	Jn 2:21; Ro 12:4-5; 1Co 6:19-20
Bosom	Place of love, affection, intimacy	Lk 16:22; Jn 1:18; 13:23
Breast	Love, intimacy, relationship	As above
Breath	Impartation of life	Ge 2:7; 7:15; Eze 37:9; Jn 20:22
Ears	Channel to receive faith	Mt 13:9,15,16,43; Ro 10:17
Eyes	Sight, insight, vision	Da 10:6; Rev 1:14
Feet	Place of humility, lowliness, walk	Lk 1:79; Ro 10:15; Heb 12:13; Rev 1:17
Feet on earth/sea	Formal possession	Ge 13:17; Jos 1:3; Rev 10:2

SYMBOL	INTERPRETATION	SCRIPTURES
Feet on neck	Victory over enemies	Jos 10:24-26
Forehead	Mind, memory, thoughts, reason, imagination	Ex 28:38; Rev 17:5; 13:16
Hair	Woman's glory	1Co 11:15
Hair (white)	Wisdom, Ancient of days	Da 7:9; Rev 1:14
Hand	Service, ministry, worship	Ps 134:2; 1Ti 2:8
Hand (left)	Judgment	Mt 25:33
Hand (right	Blessing	Mt 25:33
Heel	Crushing power, victory	Ge 3:15; Ps 41:9; Jn 13:18; Ro 16:20
Man	Image of God, intelligence, King of creation	Ge 1:26-27; Ps 8
Offspring (David's)	Humanity of Jesus, David's son	Mt 1:1; Rev 22:16
Reins	Motives of the heart	Ps 26:2; Rev 2:23
Remnant of seed	Faithful few, remaining ones	Isa 1:9; Mic 5:3; Ro 9:27; Rev 12:17
Shoulder	Place of strength, support, government	Isa 9:4, 22:22; Ex 28:12

II.   SYMBOLIC OBJECTS - MAN-MADE

SYMBOL	INTERPRETATION	SCRIPTURES
Altar	Place of sacrifice Place of incense	Ex 27:1-8; Rev 6:9 Ex 30:1-10; Rev 8:3
Anchor	Believer's security	Heb 6:19-20
Apparel	Man's need of covering; Coats of skin	Ge 3:9-11, 21; Isa 63:1-3
Ark (Noah)	Safety, salvation from death	Ge 6:14-22

SYMBOL	INTERPRETATION	SCRIPTURES
Ark (God's)	Place of glory, mercy	Ex 25:10-22
Armor	Divine equipment for warfare	Eph 6:10-12; Ro 13:12
Arrow	Suffering, conviction, the Word of God sent	Ps 38:2; 45:5; Job 6:4; Hab 3:9
Awl	Ear-mark for love-slave	Ex 21:1-6
Axe	Instrument of work, judgment	Isa 10:15; Mt 3:10
Balances	Instrument to weigh things or mankind, scarcity	Ps 62:9; Job 31:6; Da 5:27; Rev 6:2
Banner	Standard lifted up high	Isa 13:2
Barns	Man's storehouse for future	Lk 12:18, 24
Basket	Provision for man's needs	Mt 15:37; 16:9,10
Beam	Rafter of wood, or iron	Mt 7:3
Bed	Place of rest, sleep	Ps 41:3
Bell	Sweet sound of voice	Ex 28:33
Brass	Judgment against sins of disobedience	Lev 26:19; Nu 21:9; Dt 28:23
Bread	Staff of life, Christ our food	Jn 6:35; 1Co 11:23-24
Breastplate	Protection of faith and love	Isa 59:17; Eph 6:14
Bricks/slime	Human works for Babel Tower	Ge 11:3
Chain	Bondage, darkness, Satan bound	2Pe 2:4; Rev 20:1-2
Chariots	Transportation	Ge 50:9
Cistern	Man's hewn-out water-hole	Jer 2:13

SYMBOL	INTERPRETATION	SCRIPTURES
City	Permanency, security, stability	Heb 11:9-10, 16; Rev 21:1-3
Cloak	Protection from weather	Mt 5:40; 2Ti 4:13
Closet	Secret place of prayer	Mt 6:6
Cord (Scarlet)	Thread of blood atonement	Jos 2:18-21
Cup	Fullness of joy or judgment	Ps 16:5; 23:5; Jer 25:15-29; 1Co 10:16
Cymbal	Instrument of joy	1Ch 13:8; Ps 150:5
Door	Christ our entrance to life, truth, to the Father	Jn 10:2,7,9
Eyesalve	Anointing of Holy Spirit, healing for eyes	1Jn 2:20,27; Rev 3:18
Flour (Fine)	Crushing, refinement, perfect humanity of Christ's offering	Lev 2:1
Fortress/Tower	Protection, safety	2Sa 22:2; Ps 61:3; Jer 6:27
Furnace	Trial, affliction, pressure	Dt 4:20; Isa 48:10; Da 3:11
Garment/Defiled	Covering (defiled by dirt) Fleshly defilements	Isa 61:3, Mk 16:5; Jude 23; Rev 3:4
Hammer	The Word of God, crushing	Jer 23:29
Harp	Instrument of praise, worship, prophetic spirit	Ps 33:2; 71:22; 1Ch 25:1; Rev 14:2; 15:2
Helmet	Protection for head, mind	Eph 6:17; 1Th 5:8
House	The Lord's church, dwelling	Heb 3:2-6; 1Pe 2:5
Iron	Judgment against sin Inflexibility of rule	Lev 26:19; Dt 28:23 Rev 2:27; 12:5

SYMBOL	INTERPRETATION	SCRIPTURES
Lamp	Word of God Spirit of man Spirit of God	Ps 119:105 Pr 20:27 Rev 4:5
Linen (Fine)	Purity, holiness, righteousness of saints, sinless humanity	Rev 15:6; 19:8-14
Loaves (Three)	Fullness of Godhead as bread	Lk 11:5
Manna	Divine food, life, health	Ex 16:33, Jn 6:31, 49,58; Rev 2:17
Nail	Christ or Antichrist	Isa 22:22-25
Net	Gospel power to catch souls	Mt 4:18-19; 13:47-50
Ointment	Unction, oil of the Spirit	Ex 30:25; 1Jn 2:20, 27
Pillar	Support, stability, security	1Ti 3:15; Rev 3:12
Plumbline	Divine measuring standard	Amos 7:7-8
Rod	Measuring and judgment	Ps 2:9; Eze 42:15-20; Rev 11:1-2
Sieve	Divine sifting	Amos 9:9
Sickle (Sharp)	Instrument of reaping the harvest, The Word of God	Joel 3:13; Mk 4:26-29; Rev 14:14-19
Soap	Cleansing from sin	Mal 3:2
Staff	Shepherd's protection	Ps 23:4
Stone (Corner)	Christ from whom the building is aligned	Ps 118:22; Eph 2:20-21; 1Pe 2:6,7
Sword (Twoedged)	Word of God used by the Spirit	Eph 6:17; Heb 4:12; Rev 1:16; 19:15
Tent	Covering for pilgrims and strangers	Ge 13:3-18; Jer 10:20
Throne	Sovereignty of God, King of Kings, Lord of Lords	Ps 45:6; Rev 3:21; 4:2-5

SYMBOL	INTERPRETATION	SCRIPTURES
Tower	Safety, Name of the Lord	Ps 18:2; Pr 18:10
Trumpet	Prophetic voice, utterance	Nu 10:1-10; Isa 58:1; Rev 1:10; 4:1
Well	Waters of salvation, eternal life	Isa 12:2,3; Jn 4:14
Wheel	Speed, Divine transportation	Isa 5:28; Eze 1:15-21
Window	Light, illumination, blessings of heaven	Ge 6:16; Jos 2:18-21; Mal 3:10

III.   SYMBOLIC OBJECTS - MINERAL

SYMBOL	INTERPRETATION	SCRIPTURES
Brimstone	Judgments of God	Isa 30:33; Rev 9:17-18; 14:10
Dust	Frail human nature Multitude of earthly seed	Ge 18:27; Ps 103:14; Ge 13:16
Emerald	Glory of God or the saints	Rev 4:3; 21:19
Jasper	Glory of God	Rev 21:11, 18, 19
Jewels	Glories of the saints	Isa 61:10; Mal 3:17
Mire	Filth of man's works, walk	Ps 69:2, 14
Mountain	Kingdom of God, or the world	Isa 2:1-5; Rev 21:10; Da 2:45
Oil	Holy Spirit anointing	1Sa 16:13; Ps 23:5; 89:20; 1Jn 2:20, 27
Oil and Wine	Harvest of Tabernacles	Hos 2:8; Rev 6:6
Pearl	Precious truths, values Formation through suffering	Mt 7:6 Mt 13:45-46; Rev 17:4
Rivers	Flow of the Spirit of God	Jn 7:37-39

SYMBOL	INTERPRETATION	SCRIPTURES
Rocks Stones	Christ, the foundation Believers in Christ	Mt 16:18; Ps 18:2; 1Co 10:4; 1Pe 2:4-8
Salt	Enduring covenant Grace of Christ Influence of saints	Lev 2:13 Col 4:6 Mt 5:13
Salt (Savorless)	Judgment on land and people	Ge 19:26; Dt 29:23
Sand	Earthly, natural, national, seed of Abraham, multitudinous mankind	Ge 22:17; 32:12; Ro 9:27; Rev 13:1
Sea/Waves/Foam	Restless masses of humanity	Isa 57:20; Jude 13
Silver	Price of a soul Redemption money	Ex 30:11-16; Mt 27:3-9
Slime-pit	Places, mire of sin	Ge 14:10
Smoke	Presence of God in blessing or in judgment	Ge 19:28; Ex 19:18; Isa 6:4
Stones (Precious)	Glories of tribes of Israel	Ex 28:17-21; Rev 21:10-21
Vapor	Transitoriness of life	Jas 4:14

IV. SYMBOLIC OBJECTS - OBJECTS IN THE SKY

SYMBOL	INTERPRETATION	SCRIPTURES
Cloud(s)	Shekinah Glory of God Chariots of God Hosts of people, good or evil	Ex 14:19,20; 40:35; Nu 9:15-22; Isa 19:1; Ps 104:3; Heb 12:1,2; Jude 12
Light	Christ and His church	Jn 1:4-9; Mt 5:14
Rain	Revival, refreshing, outpoured Word and Spirit	Dt 32:1-2; Joel 2:23-32; Jas 5:7
Rainbow	Covenant seal of God to earth and mankind	Ge 9:12-17; Rev 4:3; 10:1

SYMBOL	INTERPRETATION	SCRIPTURES
Star(s)	Light bearers Spiritual seed of Abraham Spirit-filled leaders Glories of the resurrection	Ge 1:16-17; Mt 24:29 Ge 15:5 Rev 1:16, 20 1Co 15:41,43
Star(s) (Fallen)	Apostates, antichrist	Jude 13; Rev 9:1; 12:4
Star (Morning)	Morning light - Christ	2Pe 1:9; Rev 2:28
Sun	Glory of God the Father on Christ and/or His saints	Ps 84:11; Mal 4:2; Mt 13:43; Rev 1:16; 10:1
Sun, moon, stars	Lights of the world Glory of the Godhead and ressurrection of the saints	Ge 1:14-19; Mt 24:29; 1Co 15:41; Rev 12:1; 21:23-24
Wind	Spiritual powers, good or evil	Da 7:2,3; Ac 2:2; Eph 4:14

V.   SYMBOLIC OBJECTS - SUPERNATURAL OBJECTS

SYMBOL	INTERPRETATION	SCRIPTURES
Arm of Lord	God the Father	Isa 63:5; Jer 32:17; Isa 59:16
Book of Life	Register of heaven	Rev 3:5; Heb 12:23
Bush, burning	Son of Man, root out of dry ground	Ex 3:1-6
Chariots of fire	Divine transportation	1Ki 2:11,12
City, foursquare	Most holy place, holiest of all	Rev 21:10, 11, 16
Cloud and Pillar of fire	Christ, leader and guide to heaven	Ex 13:21,22; 1Co 10:1-2
Crown of life	Eternal life	Rev 2:10; Jas 1:12
Crown of Gold	Royalty, throne reigning	Rev 4:4; Ps 21:3
Cup, golden, of abominations	Evil communion table	1Co 10:19-21; Rev 17:4
Darkness, outer	Great tribulation, eternal state	Mt 8:12; 22:13

SYMBOL	INTERPRETATION	SCRIPTURES
Door in heaven	Access to heavenly places	Jn 1:51; Rev 4:1
Dragon, red	The devil, the serpent	Rev 12:3,9; 20:2
Eyes, full of	Sight, perfection of insight Omniscience	Eze 1:18; Rev 4:6 2Ch 16:9
Eyes, seven	Omniscience, perfection	Zec 3:9; Rev 5:6
Feet as brass	Judgment against sin of disobedience	Dt 28:23; Rev 1:15; 2:18
Finger of God	Spirit of God	Dt 9:10; Ex 8:19; Lk 11:20
Fire from mouth	Judgments of God, fiery law	2Ki 1:5-12; Rev 11:5
Flood (out of serpents mouth)	Armies, lies, Satan's propaganda	Isa 59:19; Rev 12:15, 16
Garment of glory	Christ, heavenly priest, in His glory	Ex 28:1-4; Heb 3:1; 4:14, 15; Rev 1:13
Girdle, golden	Priestly service	Ex 28:40, 41; Rev 1:13; 15:6
Glory of the Lord	Christ, glory of God in bodily form	Ex 40:34, 35; Col 1:19; 2:9
Heads, seven	Seven world kingdoms of Satan	Mt 4:8; Rev 12:3; 17:3
Horns, seven	Omnipotence, full power	Rev 5:6; Mt 28:19
Horn, ten	Ten-kingdom empire of the antichrist	Rev 12:3; 13:1; 17:3-16; Da 7:7
Key of bottomless pit	Authority over spirit realm	Mt 16:19; Rev 9:1; 20:1
Key of David	Kingdom power, Davidic throne and tabernacle	Rev 2:7; Isa 22:21-22
Keys of death and hades	Authority of spirit realms	Rev 1:18
Ladder	Son of Man connecting earth to heaven	Ge 28:12; Jn 1:51

SYMBOL	INTERPRETATION	SCRIPTURES
Manna, hidden	Christ; immortality; the Word by the Spirit	Jn 6:31, 49, 58; Rev 2:17
Mark of the Beast, 666	Mark of Satan on triune man; unpardonable sin	Rev 13:15-18; 14:9-11
Name, new	Priestly revelation and insight	Ex 28:21-29; Rev 2:17
Paradise	Third heaven, most holy place	2Co 12:2-4; Rev 2:7
Pillar/Cloud	Holy Spirit guidance	Ex 13:21, 22; 1Co 10:1, 2
Rod of iron	Power over sin, unbreakable rule	Ps 2:9; Rev 2:27; 19:15
Root of David	Christ, His pre-existence	Rev 5:5; 22:16; Isa 11:1-4
Rose of Sharon	The church of Christ, beauty	SS 2:1
Sea of glass	Tranquility of God's presence	Rev 4:6; 15:2
Seal of the living God	Holy Spirit in full redemption	Eph 4:30; Rev 7:2
Seat of Satan	Satan's throne of power	Rev 2:13; 13:1-2
Stars, seven	Ministers of the churches	Rev 1:16, 20
Stars, twelve	Twelve apostles, apostolic government	Rev 12:1; 21:12-14
Temple in heaven	Heaven's true sanctuary	Heb 8:1,2; Rev 16:17
Tree of life	Eternal life	Ge 3:22; Rev 2:7; 22:2
Trumpets, seven	Feast of trumpets; judgment; prophetic word	Isa 58:1; Nu 10:1-10; Rev 8:2,6; Jos 6
Vine of earth	Reaping of godless wicked	Rev 14:19
Voice as many waters	Majestic, awe-inspiring voice of God, of Christ	Eze 43:2; Rev 1:15
Water of Life	Eternal life by the Spirit	Jn 4:13, 14; Rev 21:6; 22:17

SYMBOL	INTERPRETATION	SCRIPTURES
Wilderness, prepared of God	Place of preservation for the church	Ex 3:18; Dt 8:1-16; Rev 12:6,14
Wine of harlot's fornication	Religious deception, doctrines, practices	Isa 63:1-4; Rev 17:2
Winepress of God's wrath	Judgment of battle of Armageddon	Isa 63:1-4; Rev 14:19,20

VI.   SYMBOLIC OBJECTS - VEGETABLE

SYMBOL	INTERPRETATION	SCRIPTURES
Almond	Fruitfulness	Nu 17:8
Aloes	Fragrance of nature	Ps 45:8; SS 4:14
Balm	Healing ministry	Jer 8:22; 46:11
Barley	Israel's Passover harvest	Ru 1:22
Bramble	Fruitless, selfish person	Jdg 9:14; Isa 34:13
Branches	The believer, the church	Jn 15:1-6
Branches, palm	Tabernacles rejoicing	Lev 23:39-44; Jn 12:13; Rev 7:9
Briar	The curse	Isa 5:6
Cassia	Fragrance of Christ	Ps 45:8
Cedar	The royal tree	1Ki 9:11
Chaff	Unnecessary, destroyed when wheat is mature, the wicked	Ps 1:4; Mt 3:12
Cinnamon	Fragrance of the world	Ex 30:23; Pr 7:17; Rev 18:13
Cluster (grapes)	Group of believers	Isa 65:8
Corn	Word of God, the food	Ps 78:24
Corn, wine, oil	Fullness of God's blessing	Dt 11:14; 14:23
Cud, chewing	Meditation in the Word	Dt 14:6-8
Cummin	Seed truths of the Word	Isa 28:25-28

SYMBOL	INTERPRETATION	SCRIPTURES
Eden	Paradise of God in earth	Ge 2:8; Isa 51:3; Joel 2:3
Field	The world	Mt 13:24-32
Fig leaves	Self-made coverings	Ge 3:1-8
Fir tree	The stately tree	1Ki 5:10; 2Ki 19:23; Isa 14:8
Flax	Weakness of man	Mt 12:20
Flower	Failing beauty of man	Jas 1:10; 1Pe 1:24
Gourd	Product of the earth	Jnh 4:6-10
Grapes	Fruit of the vine	Isa 5:2
Grass	Failing glory of man	Isa 40:6-8; 1Pe 1:24
Herb	Food of the earth	Ge 1:11, 12, 29, 30
Herb (bitter)	Sufferings of the earth	Nu 9:11; Ex 12:8
Honey	Sweet Word of God	Ps 119:103; Rev 10:9, 10
Leaven	Sin, false doctrine, hypocrisy	Lk 12:1
Leeks, garlic, onions	Food of world system	Nu 11:5
Lily of valley	The church in Christ	SS 2:1
Mustard seed	Purity of faith	Mt 13:31; 17:20
Myrrh	Suffering of death	Mt 2:11; Mk 15:23
Myrtle tree	The beautiful tree	Isa 55:13
Olive tree	Anointing or oil tree; natural Israel, or the church	Ex 30:24; Ro 11:17-24
Palm tree	The upright, fruitful tree	Ps 92:12; Jer 10:5
Palms, seventy	Seventy disciples of Christ	Ex 15:27; Lk 10:10-20
Pomegranate	Joyful and fruitful tree	Joel 1:12
Rod, Aaron's	Christ's eternal priesthood	Nu 17 with Heb 7

SYMBOL	INTERPRETATION	SCRIPTURES
Root	Christ, the foundation	Pr 12:12; Rev 22:16
Seed	The Word of God	Mt 13:3-23
Tares	Degenerates, apostates	Mt 13:25-40
Thorns/thistles	The curse on earth	Ge 3:18
Tree	Christ, believers, sinners	Ps 1:3; Da 4; Rev 2:7
Trees, two olive	Two witnesses of Christ; two anointed ones	Zec 4:3, 12, 14; Rev 11:4
Vine	Natural Israel, or Christ and His church	Ps 80; Jn 15:1-15
Vineyard	Israel, the Kingdom of God, the church; bringing forth fruit unto God	Isa 5:1-5; Mt 21:33-44

CHAPTER THREE

SYMBOLIC CREATURES

The patriarch Job said: "But ask now the <u>beasts</u>, and they shall teach thee; and the <u>fowls</u> of the air, and they shall tell thee: Or speak to the <u>earth</u>, and it shall teach thee: and the <u>fishes</u> of the sea shall declare unto thee. Who knoweth not in all these that the hand of the Lord hath wrought this? In whose hand is the soul of every living thing, and the breath of all mankind." (Job 12:7-10)

Certainly Job is not telling us to talk actually to these creatures or earth. However, he is telling us that we may learn from these creatures that God has created, as well as the earth. The lessons at times are <u>specific</u>, otherwise they are <u>implied</u>.

The Symbolic Principle is simply following out what Job exhorts us to do in this passage. Beasts, fowls, fish and the earth -- all have something to say to mankind. Creation reveals there is a Creator. The very nature, and difference in the animal kingdom teaches us many, many lessons. This is God's purpose, partly, in the creation of the animal kingdom. God created the animals and He brought them to Adam to name. The name is according to the nature of the animal (Ge 2:19-20).

I.   SYMBOLIC CREATURES

SYMBOL	INTERPRETATION	SCRIPTURES
Adder (serpent)	False teachers, causing apostasy	Ge 49:17; Ps 140:3; 58:4; Pr 23:32
Ant	Industrious, wisdom in the preparation for the future	Pr 30:25; 6:6-8
Animal parts Head/legs/fat/kidney, etc.	Inward parts of human nature	Ps 51:6; Lev 1:8-9; Ex 29:22; Lev 3:14-17
Ass (donkey)	Lowliness, patience, strength, endurance, service	Ge 49:14; Zec 9:9; Mt 21:5-7

SYMBOL	INTERPRETATION	SCRIPTURES
Ass (wild) Mule	Untamed human nature, stubborn, self-willed, unsubdued, depraved	Ge 16:12 (implied); Jer 2:24; Job 6:5; 39:5, Ps 32:9; 104:11
Asp (as adder)	False teachers	Ro 3:13; Job 20:1-16; Dt 32:33
Badger skins	Protection from storms	Ex 25:5; Eze 16:10
Bear	Evil, cunning, cruel, strong and ferocious men	2Sa 17:8; Pr 17:12; Da 7:5; Rev 13:2; 2Ki 2:24
Bees	Produce sweetness, power to sting, a host of people	Dt 1:44; Jdg 14:8; Ps 118:12
Bird (unclean)	Evil spirits, usually unclean	Rev 18:2; Mt 13:32; Jer 4:25
Blood	Life of all flesh, atonement for the soul	Ge 4:10; 9:6; Lev 17:11-14; Mt 27:25; Ps 58:10
Bullock (ox)	Strength, labor of servant, Christ, His apostles, disciples, sacrifice, burden bearing	Pr 14:4; Ps 144:14; 22:12; 1Co 9:9; 1Ti 5:18; Nu 7:88; Am 6:12
Burnt offering	Christ's voluntary offering of Himself, believers as living sacrifices	Heb 9:11-14; 10:5-7; Ps 40:6-8; Php 2:8; Ro 12:1-2
Calf	Prayers, praise, thanksgiving of our lips, skipping	Hos 13:2; Heb 13:15 with Hos 14:2
Camel	Burden-bearer, servant	GE 24:10,31,32
Cockatrice (viper)	Evil deeds, evil spirits	Isa 59:5 (vs 1-8)
Colt	Stubborness, burden-bearer	Ge 49:11; Mk 11:2
Conies	Wisdom, ability to hide in safety	Pr 30:24-26; Ps 104:18
Crane	Twitterer, lonely	Isa 38:14; Hos 7:11

SYMBOL	INTERPRETATION	SCRIPTURES
Dog	Unbelievers, unclean, evil workers	Php 3:2; Ps 22:16, 20; Pr 26:11; 2Pe 2:22; Mt 7:6; Rev 22:15
Dove(s)	Holy Spirit, gentleness, sacrifice	Mt 3:16; 10:16; Lev 1:14-17; Jn 1:32
Dragon (monster)	Satan and his cohorts, Antichristal forces	Rev 12:7, 9; 20:2; 16:1; 13:2-4
Eagle	Swiftness of flight, exchange of strength	Job 9:26; Dt 28:49; Pr 23:5; 30:19; Rev 12:14; Isa 40:31; Ps 103:5
Feathers	Covering, protection, flight	Ps 91:4; Eze 17:3, 7; Da 4:33
Fish	Souls of men, clean or unclean	Mt 4:19; Eze 47:9-10
Fat	Inward part of offering, inward warmth, health, energy, prosperity	Lev 7:1, 30-31; Ex 29:3; Ps 37:20; 92:14; 17:10; Dt 32:15
Flock	God's people in gathering	Isa 40:11; Jn 10:16 (one fold)
Fowl (unclean)	Spirit beings, usually evil (Refer to Bird)	Rev 18:2, Mk 4:32
Fox	A burrower, cunning, sly and evil men, suck blood of lambs	Lk 13:32; Eze 13:1-4; SS 2:15
Frog	That which leaps, croaks, demons or evil spirits, uncleanness	Rev 16:13; Ps 78:45; Ex 8:1-15
Grasshopper (Locust)	Smallness of size, multitude to destroy	Jdg 6:5; Nu 13:33; Jdg 7:12; Isa 40:22; Am 7:1; Mal 3:17
Goat(s)	Christ, our sin offering, unredeemed sinners	Ex 25:4 with Lev 16:15; Mt 25:32-33
Hare	Unclean, Satan and his evil spirits	Lev 11:6; Dt 14:7
Hawk (unclean)	Refer to Bird, unclean	Lev 11:13,16

SYMBOL	INTERPRETATION	SCRIPTURES
Hen	One who gathers, motherhood	Mt 23:37; Lk 13:34
Hind (deer)	Swiftness, agility, beauty	2Sa 22:34; Ps 18:33; Hab 3:19; SS 2:17; Isa 35:6
Horse	Strength, swiftness, power, spiritual support, or power of the flesh	Ps 32:9; Jer 8:6; Ps 66:12; Job 39:19; Zec 10:3; Rev 19:19
Jawbone	Strength of power under God	Isa 30:28; Jdg 15:16; Job 29:17; Eze 29:4
Kidney (reins)	Inner drives and motives of the heart	Pr 23:16; Job 16:13; 19:27; Ps 16:7; 26:2
Kine (heifer, cow)	Prosperity, wealth, milk foods and products	Dt 7:13; Ge 41:2,26,29; Am 4:1, Dt 28:4; 2Sa 17:29
Lion	Kingship, royalty, rulership, strength, courage, boldness, good or evil persons	Rev 5:5; 1Pe 5:8; Jdg 14:18; 1Sa 1:23; 2Sa 17:10; Pr 28:1; Ge 49:9; Nu 24:9; Hos 13:8
Locust	Destructive enemies and evil spirits	Na 3:17; Isa 33:4; Rev 9:3,7
Lamb(s)	The lamb of God, Jesus our sacrifice; young believers	Ex 12; 1Pe 1:19; Jn 1:29, 36; Isa 53:6; Isa 40:11
Meal offering	God's food for man	Lev 2:1; Isa 28:28
Meat	Strong truths of Word of God for the mature, spiritual food, doing the will of God	1Co 3:2; Heb 5:12-14; Jn 4:34
Milk	Foundational food and truths of God's Word, First principles	1Co 3:2; Heb 5:12-14; Isa 28:9-13; 1Pe 2:2
Moth	Destructive powers of earth, eaten with holes	Job 13:28; 27:18; Ps 39:11; Isa 50:9; 51:8; Mt 6:19-20; Lk 12:33; Jas 5:2
Owl	Night bird, evil spirits or demonic powers, wisdom	Isa 13:21; 34:13; 43:20; Jer 50:30; Job 30:29

SYMBOL	INTERPRETATION	SCRIPTURES
Peace offering	Christ our Peace-maker between God and man	Lev 3; Col 1:20; Jn 16:33; 14:27; Ro 16:20; Eph 2:14-17
Pelican	Lonely one	Ps 102:6, 7
Ram's skin (dyed red)	Christ's consecration to the Father's will, substitution	Ex 25:5; 29:26; Ge 22:13-14
Raven	Evil spirit, connected with famine	Isa 34:11; 1Ki 17:4-6; Ps 147:9; Lk 12:24; Pr 30:17
Sacrifice	Slaughter, propitiation, reconciliation, ransom, redemption	Lev 1,2,3,4,5,6,7; Heb 10:4-10; Ps 40:6-8; 2Co 5:21; Tit 2:14; 1Ti 2:5; Isa 53:7; Jn 10:18; Eph 5:2
Scapegoat	(Refer to Goat)	
Scorpion	A scourge, a whip, that which stings, brings pain, usually Satanic	Rev 9:5,10; Dt 8:15; 1Ki 12:11; 2Ch 10:11
Serpent	Subtilty, wisdom, deception, sin, applied to Satan, Christ made sin, and wisdom of believers	Ge 3:1,14; Rev 12:9; 20:2; Jn 3:14; Mt 10:16
Sheep	Christ and the people of God	Ac 8:32; Ps 79:13; 95:7; 100:3; Mt 9:36; Heb 13:20; 1Pe 2:25; Jn 10:1-11
Sin offering	Christ our Sin-bearer	Lev 4,5; 1Pe 2:24; 2Co 5:21; Gal 3:13; 1:4; Isa 53:5-10; Eph 5:2
Sow (swine, pig)	Ignorance, hypocrisy, religious unbelievers, unclean people	Mt 7:6; 2Pe 2:22; Pr 11:22; Isa 66:3
Sparrow	Small value, of little note	Mt 10:29-31; Lk 12:6-7; Ps 102:7
Spider	Activities and shrewdness of the wicked	Pr 30:28; Isa 59:5; Job 8:14

SYMBOL	INTERPRETATION	SCRIPTURES
Swallow	Wanderer from the nest, flitterer	Pr 26:2
Turtledove	(Refer to Dove)	
Unicorn (Wild bull)	Strength, power of rulers in authority	Nu 23:22; 24:8; Dt 33:17; Job 39:9-10; Ps 92:10; 22:21
Viper (serpent)	Hissing, Satan and hosts and religious leaders	Job 20:16; Isa 30:6; 54:5; Ac 28:3
Vulture	Unclean bird, evil spirits or demonic powers	Lev 11:13-14; Isa 34:15; Job 28:7
Wings	Swiftness, defense, strength, protection, flight	Ps 17:8; Ex 19:4; Dt 32:11; Isa 40:31; Mal 4:2; 2Sa 22:11; Ps 91:4; Mt 23:37; Rev 12:14
Wolf	Satan, wicked and false teachers, wolfish characteristics, who destroy God's flock	Eze 22:27; Jer 5:6; Jn 10:12; Mt 10:16; Ac 20:29; Lk 10:3; Mt 7:15; Zep 3:3
Worm (maggot)	That which is despised, also used as instrument of judgment	Mk 9:44-48; Mic 7:17; Ps 22:16; Job 25:6; 7:5; Isa 14:11; Ac 12:23; Ex 16:20

There are many other creatures listed in the Scriptures. This list is by no means exhaustive. The student is referred to G.S. Cansdale's textbook, **All The Animals of the Bible Lands** (Zondervan) for fuller treatment on Bible creatures.

From his textbook, we condense and adapt some thoughts from his "Table of Contents". G.S. Cansdale groups animals and birds of Bible lands into the following categories:

A.   Domestic Animals
Goats, sheep and oxen - all cloven-hoofed animals, clean animals generally speaking, and used for domestic purposes. Such provided milk, wool, and service for mankind. Each were animals who chewed the cud. Thus they provided food and clothing and

help for mankind. All such animals point to Christ and His people in their various natures and characteristics. Such were used for the sacrificial altar of God.

B.   Beasts of Burden
The camel, donkey, horse and mule were all beasts of burden, serving mankind in his many needs. The Lord forbad the amassing of horses in Israel because of the danger of Israel trusting in the strength of the horse and not in the Lord in the day of battle (Dt 17:16; 1Sa 8:11; Ps 32:9). Such animals point, in their positive aspects, to the strength of Christ in His saints. But the main point is burden-bearing.

C.   Beasts of the Chase
Wild ox, Desert ox, Mountain sheep, Wild goat, Deer and Gazelle; also the Wild ass. Such were beasts of the chase, they were hunted for meat as well as clothing and a range of tools and useful objects. Such wild beasts speak of untamed mankind, representing the wild, unsubdued nature of the unregenerate. This would be the main lesson learned from these beasts. They speak of the wicked, the rebellious, who God will in due time judge.

D.   Beasts - Unclean and Great
Wild and domesticated swine, all counted unclean animals and forbidden by the Lord to be eaten, and absolutely never offered on the altar of God. Totally unfit symbol of the pure, sinless body and blood of Christ's sacrifice. Isa 65:4; Pr 11:22; Isa 3:21 RSV; Mt 8:30; 7:6; Pr 26:11; 2Pe 2:22.

Other animals spoken of are Behemoth (most expositors speak of it as the Hippopotamus (Job 40:15-24), and the Elephant (1Ki 10:22; 2Ch 9:21) from which much ivory came into the kingdom of Israel in the days of Solomon. 2Ch 9:17; Am 3:15; 6:4.

No such animals were used for God's altar. The elephant was used for service once tamed, and also in warfare, as war elephants.

E. Beasts of the Cat Family
    Lion, Leopard, Cheetah, and other cats are spoken of in Scripture, either specifically or by the Hebrew Concordance. Some of the references are Ps 34:10; 17:12; Nu 24:9; Eze 19:2, Na 2:12; 1Ki 13:26; 20:35-36; 2Ki 17:25-26; Hos 13:7; Jer 5:6; Hab 1:8. Note also 2Ti 4:7.

    As noted, the lion is by interpretation, the King of the Beasts. However, in its application, it is applied to Christ, the Devil, rulers, believers as well as nations. Again, it, along with the others of the cat family, were never used for God's altar. But lions, especially, have their symbolic use, as well as other animals. This is seen in the nature of the beasts.

F. Other Beasts of Prey
    The Bear, Wolf, Dog, Fox, Jackal, Hyena, Weasel, Badger and Mongoose are the animals listed under this grouping.

    Their very natures are beastly, carnivorous, cruel, sly, cunning and were never used for God's altar. In the Scriptures we see those that are specifically named, others implied, and such are used as symbols of nations, of unregenerate and wicked people, manifesting the cruel, cunning nature of Satan and sin. These things would be the point of comparison in interpreting the symbol. 1Sa 17:34; 2Ki 2:24; Pr 28:15; Isa 59:11; Rev 13:2; Da 7:1-10; Jn 10:12; Ge 49:27; Jer 5:6; Eze 22:27; Mt 7:15; Isa 65:25. Refer also to Pr 26:11; 2Pe 2:22; Ecc 9:4; Dt 23:18; Job 30:1; Isa 56:10; Mk 7:28.

G. All Manner of Beasts
Coney, Hare, Mouse, Hedgehog, Porcupine, Mole-rat, Bats, Ape and Whales are other animals listed by G.S. Cansdale.

Such are basically unclean animals. They speak of unclean spirits, or unclean persons. Basically they are forbidden by the Lord to be eaten and certainly none were fit for God's altar. Their unclean natures did not point to the sinless and uncorrupted nature of Christ, nor to His saints. This is the major point for comparison in the use of this principle here. Pr 30:26; Lev 11:6; Dt 14:7; 1Sa 6:4.

H. Bird of Prey
Eagles, Vultures, Osprey, Buzzard, Kites, Falcons, Hawks and Owls are the birds of prey listed also. Only by checking a concordance and other tools of research can one be reasonably sure of some of these birds, or their species. Basically, these are birds of prey and are carnivorous, therefore not fit for God's altar or for food for the Hebrew nation. Most of them live on dying animals, carry infection, and God's prohibition was on the grounds of hygiene. These birds were scavengers. Some of these birds are used in a certain positive sense and other times in the negative. One has to discover what positive aspect is applied or not.

Read Ex 19:4; Dt 32:11; Ps 103:5; Job 39:27-30; Lev 11:13, 18; Dt 28:49; Hab 1:8; Jer 49:16; 12:9; Isa 40:31.

I. Birds of Passage
Pelican, Storks and Cranes are listed under this grouping. These birds are birds of migration, birds of passage. Ex 16:13; Jer 8:7; Ps 102:6; Isa 34:11; Zep 2:14; Lev 11:19; Zec 5:9; Ps 104:17; Isa 38:14; Jer 8:7. The major point of comparison is that of migration, transitoriness. This is also characteristic of some people.

J.   Fowls after their Kind
       Domestic fowls, Partridge, Quail, Peafowl, Doves and
       Pigeons are the birds listed under this grouping. It is
       difficult to settle on some of these in our day. The
       student needs to check concordances and other
       helpful tools of research.

       The Mosaic Law lists about 20 birds forbidden to be
       eaten by the Israelites and counted as unclean birds.
       Some were birds of prey, and others harder to place.
       Dt 14 needs to be read.

       In some cases, God permitted turtle doves or young
       pigeons for those who were too poor to bring a larger
       offering. Lk 2:22-24; Nu 6:10; Jn 2:11-16; Ge 8:8; Ps
       55:6; SS 2:14; Isa 38:14. The Holy Spirit is likened
       to a dove also (Mt 3:16), and Jesus told His own
       disciples to be "harmless as doves" (Mt 10:16).

       The student needs to check out the context and use
       of such to see whether it is used in a positive or
       negative sense.

K.   Birds of the Waterside
       Herons, Gulls and Terns, Kingfishers, Waders, Ducks
       and Geese are the birds listed in this grouping. Most
       of these are birds of the marshes and open waters.
       Refer to Concordance and these Scriptures. Lev
       11:17-19; Dt 14:16-18; Ps 102:16; Isa 34:11; Zep
       2:14. Some of these birds were used as a kind of
       "watch-dog" because of their cackling noises when
       disturbed, especially geese. Many of these birds
       were used for hunting, for food, for eggs for mankind.
       Again, none were used for God's altar.

L.   Birds of Every Sort
       G.S. Cansdale listed other birds also as discovered
       in Bible lands. The Raven -- Lev 11:15; Pr 30:17; SS
       5:11; Job 38:41; Ps 147:9; Isa 34:11; Zep 2:14; 1Ki
       17:4. Under the raven family or crow family are listed
       different species.

Swallows and sparrows are listed also -- Isa 38:14; Jer 8:7; Ps 84:3; Pr 26:2; Ps 102:7. Ostrich is also mentioned -- Job 39:13; La 4:3. The ostrich is a large bird and counted for its stupidity so often and its attitude to its young. Job 39:13-18. She lacks wisdom, yet she has great speed. Numerous are the lessons that these birds may teach us.

M.   Serpents in the Wilderness
Under this grouping are listed Crocodile, Lizards, Snakes and serpents of various kinds. Leviathan seems to be the crocodile -- Job 3:8; 41:1; Ps 104:25,26; Ps 74:14; Isa 27:1. There are many kinds of serpents or snakes -- Dt 32:24; Ge 3:1, 14; Nu 21:6; Isa 14:29; 30:6; Jn 3:14; Ps 140:3; Mt 3:7; 1Co 10:9; Rev 12:9; 20:2; 2Co 11:3; Mt 10:16; Lk 10:19; Mk 16:18; Ac 16:16.

All such basically refer to Satan and his demonic hosts. However, Christ was lifted up as a serpent when made sin for us. Believers are to be wise as serpents, yet harmless as doves. Frogs are spoken of as unclean spirits -- Ref 16:13.

N.   Fishes of the Sea
In Dt 14:9,10, fish that could be eaten were those having fins and scales. Any other were counted unclean by the word of the Lord. Israel as a nation was a fishing nation, especially those on the coastal regions, etc. Refer to Eze 26:5,14; Ne 13:16; Isa 19:8; Mt 4:18; 4:20; Eze 47:10; Mt 13:47; 17:27; Dt 4:18.

Fish are likened to catching the souls of men. The parable of the drag-net shows that the gospel net will gather in of all kinds, good and bad fish. The final separation comes at the coming of the Lord.

O.   Winged Creeping Things and Others
     Under this listing are Animals-without-backbones:
     Scorpion, Spider, Moth, Beetle, Flea, Fly, Gnat, Snail,
     Worm, and others.

     Read Dt 8:15; 1Ki 12:1; Lk 11:12; Isa 59:5; Job
     13:18; Isa 51:8; 1Sa 24:14; 26:20; Ecc 10:1; Isa 7:18;
     Mt 23:24; Ps 58:8; Mic 7:17; Jnh 4:7; Ac 12:23; Mk
     9:48.

     Basically all these are creatures of the earth,
     damaging, destructive and without backbone. The
     symbolic significance should be clear.

P.   Locusts, Bees and Ants
     The final grouping given in the textbook referred to
     are Locusts, Bees and Hornets, Wasps and Ants.

     Locusts are spoken of much in both the literal and
     figurative sense. Nu 13:33; Lev 11:22; Joel 2:25; Dt
     28:42; 2Ch 7:13; Am 4:9. Mostly they are
     destructive, bringing desolation to the land and all
     green trees and grass.

     They are used as symbolic of demonic forces from
     the bottomless pit (Rev 9:1-14). There were some
     kind of locusts that were suitable for food and
     permitted by the Mosaic Law. John the Baptist
     undoubtedly ate of this kind (Mt 3:4).

     Bees were a source of honey supply (Ps 81:16; Ps
     19:10; Dt 1:44; Ps 118:12). They also provided wax
     for certain uses.

     Hornets -- Ex 23:28; Dt 7:20; Jos 24:12. God used
     such to drive away enemies from the people of God.

     Ants are spoken of in Pr 6:6-8; 30:24,25. They are
     examples of industry and wisdom and speak lessons
     to indolent mankind.

II.   Conclusion

The student is reminded of the passage from Job at the beginning of this chapter. The beasts of the earth, the fowls of heaven, the fish of the sea and the earth -- all are speaking a message to mankind. Each have their distinctive traits, characteristics, nature, whether positive or negative and man may learn numerous lessons from such.

These actual creatures, created by God, teach much truth when used by God for symbolic purposes. Within the symbol is hidden truth to be discovered by those who search it out (Pr 25:2).

CHAPTER FOUR

SYMBOLIC ACTIONS

As already seen, God used various actions of men and endeavored to show to man that there was also symbolic, as well as physical significance to them. The list here notes the most important physical actions of men and briefly interprets the symbolic significance of them, whether specified or implied.

SYMBOL	INTERPRETATION	SCRIPTURES
Adultery	Violation of marriage vows, Idolatry	Eze 23:45; Jas 4:4
Anointing	Divine equipment, unction of the Holy Spirit for service	Ex 28:41; 1Jn 2:20, 27; 2Co 1:21
Awakening	Watchfulness, alertness	Isa 52:1; Eph 5:14; 1 Co 15:34
Banqueting	Feasting, festival time	SS 2:4
Baptizing	Immersion, burial of the old lifestyle	Mt 3:11; Ro 6:1-6; Col 12:12,13
Bathing	Cleansing, purification, washing	Lev 15:5; Eph 5:26; Tit 3:5
Bowing	Humility, self-abasement, worship	Ps 145:14; 146:8; Ro 11:4; Ps 95:6
Breathing	Impartation of life	Ge 2:7; Eze 37:9; Jn 20:22
Circumcising	Cutting away of filth of the flesh, covenantal seal and relationship	Ge 17:1-14; Jer 4:4; Col 2:11-13
Clapping	Joy, victory, excitement	Ps 47:1,2; 98:8
Dancing	Joy, exuberance	2Sa 6:16; Ps 30:11; Lk 15:25
Fornicating	Defilement by illicit lovers; idolatry	2Ch 21:11; Isa 23:17; Rev 17:4

SYMBOL	INTERPRETATION	SCRIPTURES
Kneeling	Worship, submission, surrender	Ps 95:6; Da 6:10; Mk 10:17; Ac 20:36
Lifting hands	Taking oath, praise, surrender	Ne 8:6; Ps 141:2; 1Ti 2:8; Rev 10:5
Marrying	Two being made one, union, covenant	Ge 2:24; Mt 19:4-6; Eph 5:31; Rev 19:7
Running	Zeal in the race of life	Heb 12:1; Isa 40:31; 1Co 9:24-26; Php 2:16
Sitting	A finished work, ceasing from labor	Ps 110:1; Heb 10:11-18; 12:2; Eph 2:6; Mk 16:17; Lk 17:7
Sleeping	Rest, refreshment, physical death, or spiritual indifference	Ac 7:60; 1Co 15:6,7; Isa 52:1; Ro 13:11; Eph 5:14
Standing	Uprightness, standing one's ground	Am 9:1; Zec 6:5; Eph 2:6; 6:13; Ps 10:1; Ac 7:55-56; Heb 10:11-12
Sweating	Human effort, activity, works, fear of suffering	Ge 3:19; Eze 44:18; Lk 22:44
Walking	Forward movement, advancement, progress	Ps 1:1-3; Isa 2:3; 40:31; 1Jn 1:7

CHAPTER FIVE

SYMBOLIC NUMBERS

Numbers, or figures, as used in the Word of God, are never used promiscuously, but take on spiritual meaning and significance. For the searcher of truth there is found to be "the treasures of wisdom and knowledge" (Col 2:3).

"It is the glory of God to conceal a thing, but the honor of kings is to search out a matter." (Pr 25:2)

All creation is stamped with "the seal of God" in numerics. God has made man a creature of Time and therefore a creature of Number! It is consistent with the very nature and being of God that His Book, the Holy Bible, should be stamped with the "seal of Bible numbers".

God is consistent throughout His Book, and though the Bible was written by various men of God over different periods of time and generations, yet there is manifest throughout all the Book the same marvelous meaning and harmony in the use of numbers. This begins in Genesis and flows through each Book of the Bible and consummates in Revelation. All this confirms the fact of Divine inspiration (2Ti 3:16; 2Pe 1:21).

I.   THE NUMERICAL PRINCIPLE

One of the principles of Biblical interpretation is the Numerical Principle. It is this principle, with its guidelines, that will help the Bible student to keep within the safety limits of Bible Numerics.

It should be remembered that there is a fine line between the significance of Bible Numerics and the danger of Numerology, the worship and idolatrous use of numbers. The student should not go beyond the boundaries of Scripture in the interpretation of numbers, whether specified or implied.

A.   Definition
The Numeric Principle has been defined as "that

principle by which the interpretation of a verse or passage in Scripture containing numbers is aided by a recognition of the symbolic significance of the numbers involved."

B.   Amplification
It is impossible to read the Scriptures without noticing the continuous use of numbers. Nearly every page of the Bible contains some usage of numbers. God Himself is the Divine numberer and He has stamped His numerical seal upon the whole of creation. This same seal has been placed upon His book -- the Holy Bible. In Da 8:13, 14, the saint who gives to Daniel the number of days concerning the cleansing of the sanctuary is referred to in a marginal rendering as Palmoni, "the numberer of secrets," or "the wonderful numberer."

Job 14:16	"For now thou <u>numberest</u> my steps..."
Ps 90:12	"So teach us to <u>number</u> our days..."
Ps 147:4	"He telleth the <u>number</u> of the stars..."
Da 5:26	"God hath <u>numbered</u> thy kingdom..."
Mt 10:30	"But the very hairs of your head are all <u>numbered</u>..."

These verses point out that God is indeed "<u>the wonderful numberer</u>." This is more particularly to be seen in His dealings with His chosen nation. Israel's way of life was governed by numbers. This was especially evident in the Tabernacle of Moses, the Feasts of the Lord, and the Ceremonial and Civil Laws (Ex 25-40).

Numbers, as used in the Word of God, are not used promiscuously, but rather take on spiritual meaning and significance. They are a special form of symbol in Scripture. There are basically two ways in which numbers are to be found in Scripture: by name (specified) and/or by implication (implied). Genesis Chapter 15 contains both of these.

Named Numbers	Verse 9	3 years
	Verse 13	400 years
	Verse 16	4 generations
Implied Numbers	Verse 9	5 sacrifices
	Verse 10	8 pieces
	Verses 19-21	10 Nations

Though the Bible was written by various men of God over many generations, there is a marvelous consistency and harmony in its use of numbers. This is because God Himself, "the wonderful numberer," was able, by inspiring the writer to shape and maintain the significance of the numbers He desired to be used.

The literary *method of numeration* used in writing Scripture gives rise to the *Numerical Principle* of interpreting Scripture.

C.   Guidelines

1.   The first step in using this principle is to recognize the numbers involved in the verse or passage, whether named or implied. The only possible difficulty in this is determining the implied numbers.

2.   The first mention of a number in Scripture generally conveys its spiritual meaning.

3.   God is consistent, and generally the significance of a number will be maintained throughout Scripture.

4.   The spiritual significance of a number is not always stated; it may be veiled or hidden. Its significance can be seen by comparing it with other Scriptures using the same number.

5.   Generally there are both good and evil, true and counterfeit, God and Satanic, aspects in the significance of numbers.

6.   The numbers from one to thirteen are the basic numbers having spiritual significance. Multiples of these numbers generally carry the same meaning, only intensifying the truth symbolized by them.

7.   This principle should be used in connection with many others, such as the First Mention, Full Mention and Symbolic Principles.

8.   This principle must be used with discretion and kept in balance with the other principles in order to avoid eccentric interpretation.

D.   Illustration (Specified & Implied)

Luke 10:1: "After these things the Lord appointed other seventy also, and sent them two and two before His face into every city and place, whither He Himself would come."

1.   **The Number Seventy**: The first number mentioned in this verse is the number seventy. By context and comparison we find that Scripture interprets the number seventy to be the number of imminent increase or representative of a multitude.

Ge 46:17	Seventy souls went down into
Ex 1:5	Egypt and there became a great nation.
Ex 24:1,9	Seventy elders represent the multitude.

In this passage the seventy disciples sent out by Christ are representative of the multitude that followed Him, and they were sent out prior to the harvest increase of disciples.

2.   **The Number Two**: The second number mentioned is the number <u>two</u>. By context and comparison we find that Scripture interprets the number <u>two</u> to be the number of testimony and witness.

Dt 19:15	One Witness is insufficient, there must be two.
Dt 17:6,7	"In the mouth of two or three witnesses shall every word be established."
Dt 19:15	"One witnesses shall not rise up...two witnesses..."
2Co 13:1	"In the mouth of two or three witnesses shall every word be established."

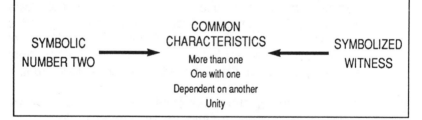

3.   **The Number Three**: The third number in this verse is there by <u>implication</u>, the number <u>three</u>. By context and comparison we find that Scripture interprets the number <u>three</u> to be the number of divine completeness and perfect witness.

Dt 17:6,7	In the mouth of two or three
2Co 13:1	witnesses shall every word be established.

In this passage each city was to receive the testimony of two witnesses. Jesus sent them into every city and place whither He Himself, the third Witness, would come. Jesus gave divine testimony and was the completion of witness.

By using the Numerical Principle this verse may be interpreted as follows: Jesus sent out the seventy disciples to represent the multitude of believers and to indicate an imminent increase. He sent them two by two because their mission was to bear witness and give testimony of Him. He purposed to follow their witness with His own perfect divine testimony.

II. THE LISTING OF BIBLE NUMBERS

Following is a brief list and interpretation of some of the numbers most often used in Scripture. These were interpreted by using the First Mention, the Progressive Mention, Full Mention and Symbolic Principles of Interpretation. The list is by no means complete and there are many shades of significance that could be added to it.

Again, the student should remember that some numbers are specified, and others are implied, as seen in the illustration. For a fuller treatment of the significance of numbers in Scripture, the reader is directed to several publications mentioned in the Bibliography.

SYMBOLIC NUMBERS

NUMBER	INTERPRETATION	SCRIPTURES
One	Number of God, Beginning, source, commencement, the first, number of compound unity (Dt 6:4: Hebrew=Echad) Numerical One (Hebrew=Yacheed)	Ge 1:1; Mt 6:33 Jn 17:21-23; Ge 2:21-24; Mal 2:14-15; Eph 2:16 Ge 22:2; Zec 12:10 with Jn 3:16
Two	Number of witness, testimony (1 with 1 = 2) Number of division, separation (1 against 1 = 2)	Jn 8:17,18; Dt 17:6; 19:15; Mt 18:16; Rev 11:2-4; Lk 9:30-31; 10:1 Ex 8:23; 31:18; Mt 7; Ge 19; Gen 1:6-8; Mt 24:40-41
Three	Number of Godhead Number of Divine completeness Perfect Testimony	1Jn 5:6-7; Mt 28:19 Dt 17:6; Mt 12:40; Eze 14:14,18; Da 3:23-24; Lev 23; Ex 12:7; 3:6
Four	Number of earth, creation, world, proceeds from three and is dependent thereon (Four winds, seasons, corners of the earth)	Ge 2:10; Lev 11:20-27; Jer 49:36; Eze 37:9; 1Co 15:39; Rev 7:1,2; Mk 13:27
Five	Number of grace, atonement, life, the cross, fivefold ministries Five "I will's" of Satan Five wounds of Jesus on cross Five in Tabernacle of Moses Five loaves - bread of life	Ge 1:20-23; Lev 1-7 (Five offerings); Eph 4:11; Ex 13:18 margin; Jos 1:14, margin; Isa 14:12-14 Ex 26:3, 9, 27,37; 27:1,18 Mk 6:38-44; Lk 9:13-16

NUMBER	INTERPRETATION	SCRIPTURES
Six	Number of man, beast, Satan, Created sixth day Six generations of Cain Six thousand years	Ge 1:26-31; 1Sa 17:4-7; 2Sa 21:20 Ge 4:17-18; Nu 35:15 (6 Cities) Ps 90;4 with 2Pe 3:8
Seven	Number of perfection, and completeness Number of Book of Revelation (Seven used about 600 times in the bible)	Ge 2:1-3; 5:24; Jude 14; Jos 6; Lev 14:7, 16, 27, 51 (The 7 Times) Rev 1:4,11,12,16,20; 2:1; 4:5; 5:1; 8:2; 10:3,4; 12:3 etc.
Eight	Number of resurrection, new beginning	Lev 14:10-23; Ex 22:30; Ge 17:12; 1Pe 3:20; Mt 28:1; Jn 20:26
Nine	Number of finality, fullness, fruitfulness Number of the Holy Spirit Number for fruit of the womb	Ge 17:1; Mt 27:45 Gal 5:22,23; 1Co 12:1-11 (9 gifts, 9 fruit of Spirit)
Ten	Number of law, order, government, restoration Antichrist kingdom Number of trial, testing and responsibility, a tithe	Ge 1: God said - 10 times Ex 34:28: Ten commandments; Da 2 (10 toes); Da 7 (10 horns); Rev 12:3 Mt 25:1-13; Lk 15:8; 19:13-25; Nu 14:22; Rev 2:10; Lev 27:32; Ex 2:3
Eleven	Number of incompleteness, disorganization, disintegration, (one beyond 10, one short of 12) number of lawlessness, disorder, the Antichrist	Ge 27:9; 32:22; Mt 20:6; Ex 26:7; Dt 1:1-8 Da 7 (The Little Horn, the 11th)

NUMBER	INTERPRETATION	SCRIPTURES
Twelve	Number of Divine Government, apostolic fullness	Ge 49:28; Ex 15:27; 24:4; 28:15-21; Mt 19:28; Lk 6:13; Rev 12:1; Lev 24:5
	Note 12 in the Holy City of God	Rev 21-22 chapters
Thirteen	Number of rebellion, backsliding, apostasy	Ge 14:4; 10:10 (Nimrod, 13th from Adam); Ge 17:25; Est 9:1; 1Ki 7:1
	Number of double portion (12 + 1 = 13)	Ge 48, Ephraim, 13th tribe; Judas or Paul, 13th apostle
Fourteen	Number of Passover (2x7=14)	Ex 12:6; Nu 9:5; Ge 31:41; Ac 27:27-33
Seventeen	Number of Spiritual order (10+7=17) ("Walk with God", the 7th and 10th man from Adam)	Ge 37:2; 1Ch 25:5; Jer 32:9; Ge 7:11; 8:4; Ge 5:24; 6:9 (Enoch/Noah)
Twenty-four	Number of priestly courses, governmental perfection (2x12=24)	Jos 4:2-9; 1Ki 19:19; 1Ch 24:3-5; 25:1-12; Rev 4:4-10 (24 elders)
Thirty	Number of consecration, maturity for ministry	Nu 4:3; Ge 41:46; 2Sa 5:4; Lk 3:23; Mt 26:15
Forty	Number of probation, testing, ending in victory or defeat	Nu 13:25; 14:33, 34; Mt 4:2; Ac 1:3; Ex 34:27,28; Eze 4:6; Ac 7:30; 1Ki 19:4-8
Fifty	Number of Pentecost, liberty, freedom, jubilee	Ex 26:5,6; Lev 25:10-11; Ac 2:1-4; Lev 23:16; 2Ki 2:7; 1Ki 18:4,13; Nu 8:25
Seventy	Number prior to increase, or representative of a multitude	Ge 4:24; 11:26; 46:27; Ex 1:5-7; Nu 11:25; Ex 15:27; 24:1,9; Lk 10:1
Seventy-five	Number of separation, cleansing, purification	Ge 12:4; Da 12:5-13 (implied)

NUMBER	INTERPRETATION	SCRIPTURES
One Hundred Twenty	Number of end of all flesh, the beginning of life in the Spirit	Ge 6:3; Dt 34:7; 2Ch 3:4; 5:12; 7:5; Ac 1:5
One Hundred Forty-four	Number of God's ultimate in creation and redemption (12x12=144)	Rev 21:17; 1Ch 25:7; Rev 7:1-6; 14:1-3
One Hundred Fifty-three	Number of God's elect, revival, ingathering, harvest (9x17=153)	Jn 21:6-11 (Fish ingathering)
Three Hundred	Number of faithful remnant	Ge 5:22; 6:15; Jdg 8:4; 15:4
Six-Six-Six	Number of Antichrist, Satan, mark of the damned, mark of the man who is a beast	Da 3; 1Sa 17; Da 7 with Rev 12:18; 14:9-11 (Note the 6's in these chapters)

(The student is referred to the following publications on Numbers in Scripture:

Bullinger, Ethelbert W., Number in Scripture, Kregel Publications

Payne, F.C., The Seal of God in Creation and The Word, Adelaide, Australia

Vallowe, Ed F., Keys to Scripture Numerics, 528 Pine Ridge Drive, Forest Park, Georgia 30050, USA

CHAPTER SIX

SYMBOLIC NAMES

In the writing of Scripture, God, who knows all men, caused the writers to write the names of numerous persons, both men and women. There are almost 2900 or so persons mentioned in the Scriptures. Some only get a passing reference, while others have whole chapters given over to their life story. In Bible times names had much more significance than they do today in our Western world and culture.

The name always speaks of the nature, the character, the office or function of a person. They did not always live up to the name, as often times it was a name that had a Godly meaning.

An illustration of a symbolic name is that of the Patriarch Job. James 5:11 tells of "the patience of Job..." The symbolic element in this verse is the name "Job". By referring to the Book of Job and other study helps we find that Job's name means "persecuted". In Scripture a name is significant and often prophetic of what a person may experience in his life time. This is true of persons and nations. Thus we determine by the context the comparison that Job's name was indicative of his experience of suffering and persecution.

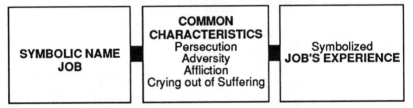

This simple analogy can be applied to numerous people mentioned in the Bible. By the interpretation of their name, and the outworking of experience in their life story, the student may learn many lessons that help to build character and strength in one's own relationship with the Lord and with others.

Balance must be taken in the application of the interpretation of a name in Scripture. Doctrines must not be built on such, but such may be used for illustration of that portion of truth that is appropriate. Names interpreted must not be forced on proper interpretation of the Scripture.

Following are a very few examples of names interpreted and the significance of the same in their historical setting.

THE NAME	INTERPRETATION	HISTORICAL SETTING	SCRIPTURE
Abel	"Transitory, mourning"	First martyr, slain by his brother Cain	Ge 4:2
Abraham	"High father of a great multitude"	Seed as sand and stars from his loins	Ge 17:5
Amalek	"A people that licks up"	Enemies of Israel of God	Ge 36:12
Apollyon	"One that exterminates, destroyer"	Satan, destroys mankind	Rev 9:11
Babel	"Confusion"	Confusion of languages	Ge 11:9
Beer-Sheba	"Well of the oath"	Covenant between Isaac and Abimelech at well	Ge 21:31
Benjamin	"Son of my right hand"	Named by father Jacob	Ge 35:18
Benommi	"Son of my sorrow"	Named by Rachel at birth	Ge 35:18
Bethlehem	"House of bread"	Birthplace of Christ, the Bread of Life	Ge 35:19; Mic 5:2
Bethel	"House of God"	Jacob meets with God	Ge 28:12:22

THE NAME	INTERPRETATION	HISTORICAL SETTING	SCRIPTURE
Ichabod	"The glory is departed"	Loss of Ark of God to the Philistines	1Sa 4:21
Jerusalem	"Foundation of Peace"	God's city in earth	Jos 10:1
Lo-Ammi	"Not My people"	House of Israel cast off	Hos 1:9
Lo-Ruhamah	"No more mercy"	House of Israel cast off	Hos 1:6
Maher-Shal-al-hash-baz	"Speeding to the spoil, he hastens to the prey"	Captivity of Israel	Isa 8:1
Peter	"A Stone"	Prophecy of Christ on Simon	Mt 16:18; Jn 1:42
Zion	"Fortress, Sunny"	Mount of David's throne and tabernacle	2Sa 5:7

The student should remember that interpreting the names should be done within the historical setting, and within the limits of Scripture. Bible names generally had some spiritual significance.

When a person had a godly name but an ungodly character, it was significant of the fact that they did not live up to their name, even as today. The converse is true also, for some godly people had sorrowful names, but they allowed God to work in their lives and turn sorrow into joy, and the negative into the positive.

CHAPTER SEVEN

SYMBOLIC COLORS

Again, we see how God, the Creator and Author of all light, all colors of light, uses various colors to communicate truth to us by way of symbolic use. Here we note the main colors mentioned in Scripture and their significance, either specific or implied.

SYMBOL	INTERPRETATION	SCRIPTURES
Amber	The glory of God	Eze 1:4; 8:2
Black	Sin, death, famine	La 4:8; Jer 8:21; Rev 6:5
Blue	Heaven, heavenly, authority, from above, Holy Spirit	Nu 15:38; Jn 14:26 (Blue hem - remind)
Crimson	Blood atonement, sacrifice or death	Lev 14:52; Jos 2:18, 21; Isa 1:18
Purple	Kingship, royalty	Jdg 8:26; Jn 19:2
Red	War, bloodshed, death	2Ki 3:22; Rev 6:4; 12:3
Scarlet	Blood atonement; sacrifice (as crimson)	Lev 14:52; Jos 2:18, 21; Isa 1:18
White	Purity, light, righteousness, holiness of God, Christ, the angels or saints	Rev 6:2; 7:9; 19:8; 3:4-5; 15:6

CHAPTER EIGHT

SYMBOLIC DIRECTIONS

In Scripture, God attributed symbolic significance to directions. Therefore, many times, beyond the geographical or physical, there is some spiritual and symbolic significance to be discovered. Such may be seen specified or implied.

SYMBOL	INTERPRETATION	SCRIPTURES
Backslide	To backslide, withdraw, or apostasy	Pr 14:14; Jer 3:6-22; Heb 10:38-39
Crooked	Twisted, distorted in the spiritual	Isa 40:3,4; Lk 3:4-5
Down	Spiritual declension, backslide, falling away, or humility and prostration	Ge 12:10; 13:1; Isa 14:12-13; Jnh 1:3,5; Lk 10:15, 30; Rev 5:8
East	Place of God's glory, the Sun-rising, Cherubim	Eze 43:1,2; Rev 7:2; Mt 24:27; Ge 3:24
North	Place of God's throne, judgments of God	Ps 75:6,7; Isa 14:12-14; Ps 48:1-3; Jer 1:13-14
North South East West	Universal, worldwide, the four corners of the earth The 12 oxen face north, south, east and west (1Ki 7:25)	Ge 28:14; Mt 8:11; Lk 13:29; Rev 21:13; Mt 28:18-20; Ac 1:8; Jer 1:14
South	Place of refreshment	Ps 126:4; SS 4:14
Straight	Spiritual progression with digression	Jn 1:23; Isa 40:3-4; Lk 3:4-5
Up	Spiritual ascension, or pride, self-exaltation	Ge 13:1; Isa 2:2-4; Lk 19:29; Pr 16:18; Isa 14:12-14
West	Sunset, setting down	Isa 59:19; Ps 103:12; Mt 8:11

CHAPTER NINE

SYMBOLIC PLACES

In Scripture, God attributed symbolic significance to various places. Again, these are either specified or implied by the various nature and character of the places mentioned. The character of the place provides the key to its interpretation when used in symbolic manner.

SYMBOL	INTERPRETATION	SCRIPTURES
Babylon	Confusion of tongues, origin of nations	Ge 11:1-9; Rev 17-18
Canaan	Inheritance of promises Spiritual warfare	Jos 14:1; Ps 105:11
Cities of Refuge	Refuge in Christ and the Church	Jos 20:1-6; Heb 6:18
Eden	Paradise of God, Delight, Garden of God, Third heaven	Ge 2:8; Isa 51:3; Joel 2:3; 2Co 12:1-4
Egypt	House of bondage, the world system, house of Satan's works	Ex 12; Dt 5:6; Ex 20:2
Gog/Magog	Godless masses of the wicked	Eze 38,39; Rev 20:7-8
Jericho	City of Palm Trees	Dt 34:3
Jerusalem	City of God and Peace	Ps 116:19; Rev 21, 22
Jordan river	Descending, going down, death to self, baptism	2Ki 5:10; Mt 3:5-6; Mk 1:9
Mt Ebal	Mount of Cursing	Dt 27:13; Jos 8:32-33
Mt Gerizim	Mount of Blessing	Dt 27:13; Jos 8:32-33
Mt Moriah	Sacrifice, substitution, the Temple site and foundation	Ge 22:2; 2Ch 3:1

SYMBOL	INTERPRETATION	SCRIPTURES
Mt Sinai	Law Covenant, Commandments, Fear, bondage, legalities	Ex 19:1-6; Heb 12:18-21;Gal 4:24-25
Mt Zion	New Covenant, throne of David, kingship, Tabernacle of David, worship and praise, priesthood	Heb 12:22-24; Rev 14:1; 1Ch 15-16; Am 9:9-15; Ac 15:15-18
Red Sea	Separation, division, baptism in water	Ex 13:18; 14:21-22; 1Co 10:1,2

CHAPTER TEN

SYMBOLS IN THE TABERNACLE OF MOSES
(As Pertaining To Christ and His Church)

As noted in Chapter One, **The Language of the Symbol**, without question the Lord intended Divine truths and spiritual realities to be represented in symbolic form in the construction of the Tabernacle of Moses, and also the Temple of Solomon.

God took of the material realm and used such materials for His dwelling place among the people of Israel. Everything primarily points to Christ first, to His person and work, and secondarily points to His saints and the Church, His Body.

The Book of Hebrews especially confirms these things by use of the Comparative Mention Principle of interpreting the Word. "In the volume of the book it is written of Me..." (Heb Chapters 5-10; Heb 10:5-7). The Word was made flesh and dwelt (Grk Lit: pitched His tent, tabernacled) among us and we beheld His glory (Jn 1:14).

Following is a list of things used in the construction and ministry of God's habitation, whether Tabernacle or Temple, and the interpretation of the symbol, whether specific or implied. For, the Psalmist said, "In His Temple doth every one (Margin KJV: "every whit of it") speak of his glory" (Ps 29:9).

SYMBOL	INTERPRETATION	SCRIPTURES
Altar of Brass	Place of slaughter, sacrifice, substitution, points to the cross	Ex 27:1-2; Heb 13:10-13
Altar of Incense	Place of intercession, mediatorship, advocate, Christ our intercessor	Ex 30:1; Heb 7:25; 1Jn 2:1; 1Ti 2:5
Ark of Covenant	Place of God's communication, place of blood propitiation, the mercy seat	Ex 25:10; Heb 9:4; 2Co 5:18-21; Ro 4:25 (Grk); Col 2:9

SYMBOL	INTERPRETATION	SCRIPTURES
Blue	Color of heaven, authority of heaven over earth, Christ the Lord from heaven	Ex 25:4; 26:1,4; 1Co 15:47
Book of Law Seven Sealed	Inspired written records, God's commands Bible, Book of Redemption	Jos 1:8; 2Ki 22:8; Dt 31:9-26; Ezr 4:15; Ne 8:1-8; Jer 25:13; Rev 1:11 Jer 32:6-12 with Rev 4,5
Brass (Copper)	Judgment against sin of disobedience, heaven as brass or iron; Christ, judge of all sin	Ex 25:3; Nu 21:9; Dt 28:13-23; Isa 4:4; Rev 1:12-15
Candlestick (Lampstand)	Place of light, illumination; Christ, light of world; Word of God is a lamp; Church is God's light	Ex 25:31-35; Jn 1:1-5; Ps 119:130; Rev 1:12-20; Zec 4:1-2; Rev 11:4
Cakes (Unleavened)	Purity of life offered to God	Ex 12:39; Jdg 7:13
Cloud of Glory Pillar of Fire	Guidance, direction, leading people of God to Canaan; Holy Spirit guidance	Ex 13:21-22; 1Co 10:1-2; Lk 1:79; Jn 16:13
Commandments on Stone Tables	The Laws of God, moral and civil; Relationships with God and man; Christ our Lawgiver	Ex 34:28; Ro 10:4; Jn 14:14,21; Mt 5,6,7; Isa 33:22
Door of Tabernacle	Place of entrance or exit, enter in and out, Christ our entrance to God	Ex 26:26; Jn 10:9; 14:1,6
Garments	Covering of nakedness, protection, warmth, office of ministry of priesthood before God	Ex 28:1-4, 40-45; Heb 3:1; 4:14-15; 9:24
Gate of Court	Place of entrance or exit, enter in or out, Christ our point of entrance to God	Ex 27:16; Jn 14:1,6
Girdle	Bound to service	Isa 11:5; Ex 28:8

SYMBOL	INTERPRETATION	SCRIPTURES
Glory of Lord	Visible manifestation of God's presence	Ex 40:34; Jn 1:14-18; Col 1:19; 2:9
Gold	God (or gods), Divine nature, glory, faith of saints	Ex 25:3; Ac 17:29; Rev 21:21-22; 1Pe 1:7; 2Pe 1:4; Job 23:10
Hair (Goat's hair, Mankind)	Covering, glory of the creature	Ex 25:4; Heb 9:12; Lev 4:22-29; Lev 16:15-16
Incense (Gold censer)	Prayer, intercession of Christ and His saints	Ex 25:6; Ps 141:1-2; Heb 7:25; Rev 5:8; 8:1-5; Lk 1:10; Ro 8:26-27
(Brass censer)	Counterfeit prayers Judged by God	Lev 16:12-13 with Nu 16:37-40
Laver (Brass)	Place of washing, cleansing for service by the Word; Sanctification by Christ	Ex 30:18; Eph 5:26 (Grk washing) Tit 3:5 (Grk washing); Jn 13:1-17
Lamps (seven)	Perfections of the Spirit	Zec 4:2; Rev 4:5; Ex 25:31-40
Candle-light	Spirit of man, God's lamp	Pr 20:27; Job 18:6; 29:3
Linen	Purity, righteousness of Christ, saints, angels, Christ our Righteousness	Ex 25:4; Rev 15:5-6; 19:8-14
Loaves (Manna) Shewbread	Heavenly food, staff of life, health, nourishment, communion, Christ our heavenly bread	Ex 16:33; Jn 6:32-51; Ex 25:23-30; 1Co 10:16,17
Loaves (two wave loaves)	Christ and His Church as bread, two yet one	Lev 23:15-21; 1Co 10:16,17
Offerings (five Levitical)	Christ our sacrifice, and offering, and oblation to God	Lev 1,2,3,4,5,6,7 chapters; Eph 5:1-2; 2Co 5:19-21
Olive oil	Anointing, unction for service, anointed ones; Christ and Christians	Ex 25:6; Jn 1:32,33,41; 4:25-26; Ac 11:26
Outer Court (unmeasured)	Tribulation saints	Rev 11:2

SYMBOL	INTERPRETATION	SCRIPTURES
Pillar in temple of God	Permanency, security, stability	Gal 2:9; Rev 3:12
Purple	Royalty, kingship, blend of blue and scarlet, the God-man, Christ our king	Ex 25:4; Jn 19:2; Mk 15:17
Raiment (white)	Priestly garment, purity, righteousness	Ex 28:39-41; Rev 3:5,18; Ps 132:9,16
Ribband (blue hem)	Reminder of God's Laws	Nu 15:38 with Jn 14:26
Robe (white)	Office, position, priestly garments, righteousness, salvation	Lev 8:1-11; Isa 22:21; 61:6,10; Rev 7:9,13,14
Rod	Priesthood, shepherdizing, leading, guiding, protection, measuring; Christ our shepherd and measuring rod	Nu 17:8; Heb 7:17; 9:4; Rev 11:1-2
Scarlet	Sacrificial color, blood shed for sin; Christ our sacrifice	Ex 25:4; Mk 15:17; Heb 9:19; Mt 27:28; Isa 1:18
Scepter	Kingship, rule, law and authority	Ge 49:10; Nu 24:17
Silver	Atonement for the soul, price of a soul, redemption; Christ our redeemer	Ex 25:3; 30:11-16; Zec 11:12-13; Mt 27:3-9; 1Pe 1:18-20
Skins (Badgers, Rams, skins dyed red)	Covering, protection; Christ our covering before God, Ram of substitution and consecration to God	Ex 25:5; Eze 16:19; Isa 52:14; 53:2; Ex 25:4; Ge 22:13; Ex 29:31
Spices	Fragrance manifested by crushings, sufferings	Ex 25:6; 30:22-38; SS 4:16
Stones (onyx and other gem stones)	Preciousness, value, glories, gifts, Preciousness of glory of Christ in His saints	Ex 25:7; 28:15-21; Mal 3:7; Pr 17:8; Rev 21:18-20

SYMBOL	INTERPRETATION	SCRIPTURES
Tabernacle	Habitation of God among His people, Heavenly dwelling of all the redeemed	Ex 40:34,35; Jn 1:14 (Grk dwelt); Heb 8:2
	The human body	2Pe 1:14; Jn 1:14
Table	Place of fellowship, feast, communion, nourishment, food	Ex 25:23-30; Lev 24:5-9; Ps 23:5; 1Co 11:23-34; Ac 2:42
Veil	Divider, separator, that which hides or conceals access to God, Christ our veil-render and access to the Father	Ex 26:31-35; Mt 27:51; Jn 14:1,6; Heb 9:1-14; 10:19-20
Vials (golden bowls)	Temple vessels, bowls, basins	1Ki 7:50; Rev 5:8; 15:7
Wave-sheaf of firstfruits	Christ's resurrection and resurrection of the saints as the harvest	Lev 7:30; 23:11-12; 1Co 15:20,23
Wood (acacia)	Incorruptible wood, non-decaying wood, humanity of Christ, Root out of dry ground, Stem of Jesse	Ex 25:5; Isa 11:1-5; Jer 23:5; Zec 6:12, The Branch

71

CHAPTER ELEVEN

SYMBOLS IN THE BOOK OF REVELATION

The book of Revelation, the last book of the Bible, "The Book of Ultimates", has many symbols therein.   There are at least 130 symbols in Revelation and without understanding them, it is virtually impossible to interpret this majestic book.

Following we list the symbols in this book. The student will note the Scripture references given where the symbol is interpreted, either specifically or by implication.

REVELATION	SYMBOL	INTERPRETATION	SCRIPTURE REFERENCES
1:10; 4:1	Trumpet	Voice of prophetic utterance	Isa 58:1; Nu 10:1-10
1:11	Book	Written inspired records	2Ki 22:8-13; Ne 8:1-17
1:12, 13	Gold candlesticks	The seven local churches	Rev 1:20
1:13	Garment to foot	Priestly clothing	Ex 28:2
1:13; 15:6	Golden girdles	Priestly service	Ex 28:40, 41
1:14	Hair white as wool	Wisdom, Ancient of Days	Da 7:9
1:14	Eyes-flame of fire	Searching, penetrating insight	Da 10:6
1:15	Feet as fine brass	Judgment against sin	Dt 28:23
1:15	Voice-many waters	Majestic, awe-inspiring	Eze 43:2
1:16	The seven stars	Seven church ministers	Rev 1:20
1:16; 19:15	Two-edged sword	Word of God by the Spirit	Eph 6:17
1:16; 10:1	The sun	Glory of God the Father	Mt 13:43

REVELATION	SYMBOL	INTERPRETATION	SCRIPTURE REFERENCES
1:18	Keys/hades & death	Authority over spirit realm	Mt 16:19
2:7	Tree of life	Eternal life	Ge 3:22
2:7	Paradise	Third heaven, most holy place	2Co 12:2-4
2:10	Crown of life	Eternal life	Jas 1:12
2:13	Satan's seat	Satan's throne of power	Rev 13:1,2
2:17	Hidden manna	Word of God by the Spirit	Jn 6:35
2:17	White stone	Priestly revelation	Ex 28:15-28
2:17	A new name	Priestly revelation, insight	Ex 28:21-29
2:22	Bed of adultery	Spiritual fornication, lusts	Jas 4:4
2:27; 19:15	Rod of iron	Power over nations	Ps 2:9
2:28	Morning star	Morning light	2Pe 1:19
3:4	Defiled garments	Garments defiled by flesh	Jude 23
3:5,18	White raiment	Priestly attire	Ex 28:39-41
3:5	Book of Life	Register of heaven	Heb 12:23
3:7	Key of David	Kingdom power	Mt 16:19; Isa 22:21-22
3:12	Pillar of temple	Stability, permanent Position	Gal 2:19
3:18	Gold tried in fire	Faith of God; divine nature	2Pe 1:7
3:18	Eyesalve	Anointing of the Spirit	1Jn 2:20,27
3:21; 4:2-5	The throne	Sovereignty of God	Ps 45:6
4:1	Door in heaven	Access to heavenly places	Jn 1:51

REVELATION	SYMBOL	INTERPRETATION	SCRIPTURE REFERENCES
4:3	Jasper/sardine stones	Glory, brightness of God	Rev 21:11
4:3; 10:1	The rainbow	Covenant of God with earth	Ge 9:12-17
4:4	Crowns of gold	Royalty, reigning on throne	Ps 21:3
4:4	Twenty-four elders	Priestly courses & ministry	1Ch 24
4:5	Lightnings, voices, thunders	Judgments of God in earth	Ex 19:16
4:5	Seven lamps of fire	Fullness of Holy Spirit	Zec 4:2
4:6	Full of eyes	Sight, perfection of insight	Eze 1:18; 2Ch 16:19
4:6-8	Four living beasts	Four standards of Israel	Eze 1:10
	The lion	King of beasts, royalty	
	The calf	Kings of domestics, sacrifice	
	The man	King of creation, intelligence	
	The eagle	King of birds, heavenliness	
5:1-7	Seven-sealed book	Bible, book of redemption	Jer 32:6-12
5:6	Slain lamb	Sacrifice, atonement, Son of God	Jn 1:29,36; Ex 12
5:6	Seven horns	Omnipotence, fullness of power	Ps 92:10
5:6	Seven eyes	Ominiscience, insight	Zec 3:9
5:8	Golden vials	Temple vessels, bowls, basins	1Ki 7:50

REVELATION	SYMBOL	INTERPRETATION	SCRIPTURE REFERENCES
5:8	Odors, incense	Prayers of saints	Ps 141:1,2
5:9	New song	Songs of redemption	Ex 15:1
5:9	Blood atonement	Calvary, redemption	Lev 17:11-14
5:10; 1:6	Kings and priests	Order of Melchizedek	Heb 7:1-3
6:2	White horse and rider	Word and Spirit of revival	Rev 19:11-21
6:4	Red horse and rider	Spirit of war	Rev 12:3
6:5	Black horse and rider	Spirit of famine	La 5:10
6:8	Pale horse and rider	Spirit of pestilence, death	Mt 24:7
6:5	Balances	Scarcity, weighing out	Job 31:6
6:6	Wheat and barley	Passover, Pentecost harvests	Hos 2:22
6:6	Oil and wine	Tabernacles harvest	Hos 2:8,22
6:9	Altar(of brass)	Place of sacrifice, life outpoured	Ex 27:1-8
7:1	Four winds of earth	Powers of evil	Da 7:2
7:2	Seal of God	Holy Spirit, full redemption	Eph 4:30
7:2	The east	Sunrise, heaven, light	Ge 3:24
7:9	Palm branches	Tabernacles of rejoicing, victory	Lev 23:39-44; Jn 12:13
7:9,13,14	White robes	Priestly garments	Ex 28:40,41
7:14	Washed white	Cleaned by blood atonement	Ex 28:4041
8:3,5	Golden censer	Intercessory prayers	Lev 16:12,13
8:3	Golden altar	Intercessory ministry	Ex 30:1-10

REVELATION	SYMBOL	INTERPRETATION	SCRIPTURE REFERENCES
8:2,6	Seven trumpets	Feast of Trumpets; judgments	Jos 6: Nu 10:1-10
8:13 (Grk)	Eagle messenger	Translated saints	Isa 40:31
9:1	Fallen star	Antichrist, apostate	Jude 13
9:1; 20:1	Key of the bottomless pit	Authority over spirit realm	Mt 16:19
9:2	Smoke from pit	Religious confusion	Ps 37;20
9:3-12	Locust armies	Demon spirits	Ex 10:1-20
9:13-21	Horsemen armies	Devil-inspired armies, Counterfeit God's armies	Compare God's armies Rev 19:11-21
10:1-7	Little open book	Book of Daniel(Biblios)	Da 12
10:2	Feet on earth/sea	Formal possession	Jos 1:2-5
10:3,4	Seven thunders	Secret sayings of God	Jn 12:27-30; Ps 29:3-9
10:5	Lifted up hand	Oath to God	Ge 14:22
10:9-11	Eating the book	Receiving Word of God	Eze 3:1-3
11:1	Reed or rod	Measuring, or judging	Eze 42:15-20
11:1,2	Temple measured	Church measured up to the standard of the Word	Eph 4:10-16
11:2	Outer court left unmeasured	Tribulation saints	Mt 5:13
11:2	Trodden under foot	Defeated, down-trodden	Lk 21:24
11:3	Sackcloth	Mourning, sorrow, judgment	Jnh 3:5-8
11:4	Two olive trees	Anointed witnesses	Zec 4:3,12,14
11:4	Two candlesticks	Light bearers	Zec 4:3,12,14

REVELATION	SYMBOL	INTERPRETATION	SCRIPTURE REFERENCES
11:5	Fire out of mouth	Fiery law, judgment of God	2Ki 1:5-12; Dt 33:2
11:19	Heavenly temple	True sanctuary of God	Heb 8:1,2
11:19	Ark of testament	Glory-throne of God	Ps 80:1; 99:1
12:1	A woman	The true church, bride of Christ	Eph 5:23-32; Rev 21,22
12:1	Sun, moon, stars	Glory of Godhead in the resurrection	Ge 1:14-19; 1Co 15:41
12:1	Twelve stars	Twelve last-day apostles	Rev 21:12-14
12:3	Red dragon	The devil, serpent, Satan	Rev 12:3,9; 20:2
12:3	Seven heads	Seven world kingdoms of Satan	Mt 4:9; Rev 11:15
12:3	Ten horns	Ten kingdom empire of the Antichrist	Da 7:7; Rev 17:3-16
12:4	Falling stars	Apostate saints, falling	Jude 13; Ge 15:5
12:6	Prepared wilderness by God	Place of preservation for the true church	Ex 3:18; Dt 8:1-16
12:14	Eagle's wings	Holy Spirit transport	Ac 8:39; Isa 40:31
12:15,16	Flood out of the serpent's mouth	Lies, armies, propaganda of Satan	Isa 59:19
12:17	Remnant of woman's seed	Remaining saints	Mt 25:1-13 (Foolish virgins left out)
13:1; 20:8	Sand of the sea	Physical, fleshly seed of humanity	Ge 13:16; 22:17
13:1	The first beast	Antichrist/his kingdom	Da 7
13:11	The second beast	The false prophet	Rev 19:20

REVELATION	SYMBOL	INTERPRETATION	SCRIPTURE REFERENCES
13:15-18	Mark of beast	Unpardonable sin; triune man in sin under Satan	Rev 14:9-11
14:1	Mt Zion	Ruling power of the Son of David's Tabernacle	Heb 12:22-24; Ac 15:15-18
14:2; 15:2	Harps	Prophetic spirit, worship	1Ch 25:1
14:14	Sharp sickle	Reaping instruments, harvest time	Mk 4:26-29
14:14	White cloud	Shekinah glory cloud	Ex 14:19,20
14:15	Harvest of earth	Reaping of His saints	Mt 13:37-43
14:19,20	Winepress of God's wrath	Armageddon	Isa 63:1-4
15:2	Sea of glass	Tranquility of God's presence	Rev 4:6
15:2	Mingled with fire	Fiery trials of tribulation	Job 23:10
15:7	Seven vials/bowls	Temple vessels poured out	1Ki 7:50
15:8	Smoke of God's glory	Blinding glory, permitting no entry	Ex 19:18
16:13	Three frogs	Unclean, evil spirits	Rev 16:13,14
17:1-7	Great harlot	The false church	Pr 7:6-23
17:1	Wine of fornication	Religion, deception, evil doctrines and practices	Isa 28:7,8
17:3	The wilderness	Godless, forsaken world	Jer 4:23-28
17:4	Golden cup of abominations	Evil communion table	1Co 10:19-21
17:9-10	Seven mountains	Seven world kingdoms of Satan	Lk 4:5-8
17:15	Waters	Peoples, nations, tongues	Rev 17:15

REVELATION	SYMBOL	INTERPRETATION	SCRIPTURE REFERENCES
18:2	Fallen Babylon	Confusion, religious and political	Ge 11:1-10
18:2	Cage of birds	Unclean and foul spirits	Rev 18:2
19:7	Marriage of Lamb	Union of Christ and Church	Eph 5:23-32
19:8	Fine linen, clean and bright	Righteousness of saints	Rev 19:8
19:9	Marriage supper	Kingdom communion time	Mt 26:26-29
19:11-16	White horse rider and armies	Christ and His saints and angels in victory	Rev 19:11-14
20:1,2	A great chain	Binding of Satan, chains of darkness	2Pe 2:4
20:8	Gog and Magog	Godless masses of the wicked resurrected dead	Eze 38,39; Rev 20:1-6
21:6; 22:17	Water of life	Eternal life by the Spirit	Jn 4:13,14; 7:37-39
22:1	River of water of life	Flowing of the Holy Spirit	Jn 7:37-39
21:16	Foursquare city of God	Most holy place, heaven's holiest of all	Rev 21:10,11,16
22:15	Dogs	Unclean, vile, unredeemed	Php 3:2
22:16	Root of David	Deity of Christ Jesus, His pre-existence, Lord	Isa 11:1-4; Ps 110:1
22:16	Offspring of David	Humanity of Jesus as David's Son	Mt 1:1; Jer 23:5,6

SECTION TWO

THE TYPICAL PRINCIPLE

It is impossible to properly and fully interpret the types in Scripture without the proper interpretation of the symbols used in the types. The language of the type includes in itself the language of the symbol. Hence we have the need of a chapter in this section pertaining to the use of the Typical Principle.

CHAPTER TWELVE

THE LANGUAGE OF THE TYPE

I.   DEFINITION

The typical principle is that principle by which the interpretation of a verse or passage of Scripture containing typical elements can be determined only through a proper interpretation of the type or types involved.

If symbols are involved (as usually they are), then the Symbolical and Typical Principles will be used together to arrive at a proper interpretation.

II.   AMPLIFICATION

    A.   Definition of Types

        Webster's Dictionary defines the word "type" as:

        An emblem; a symbol; that which has a symbolical significance; that which is emblematic.

        An allegorical symbolic representation of some object, which is called the antitype; a symbol; a sign; theologically, the word is mainly applied to those prophetic prefigurings of the persons and things of the new dispensation, which occur in the Old Testament.

        The word "type" comes from the Greek word "TUPOS", which means "The mark of a stroke or blow; a figure formed by a blow or impression; the impress of a seal, the stamp made by a die; a figure, image, form, or mold; counterpart; example to be initiated; a model, pattern; an anticipative figure."

It is translated:

1.	Print	Jn 20:25
2.	Figure	Ac 7:43; Ro 5:14
3.	Fashion	Ac 7:44
4.	Manner	Ac 23:25
5.	Form	Ro 6:17
6.	Example	1Co 10:6; 1Ti 4:12
7.	Ensample	1Co 10:11; Php 3:17; 1Th 1:7; 2Th 3:9; 1Pe 5:3
8.	Pattern	Tit 2:7; Heb 8:5

For the purposes of defining the Typical Principle now under consideration we will define a "type" to be a figure or representation of something to come; an **anticipative figure**, a **prophetic symbol**. This necessitates a brief discussion of the distinction between types and symbols.

III.   DISTINCTION BETWEEN TYPE AND SYMBOL

Types are to be viewed as a select group of symbols having prophetic and foreshadowing characteristics.

Symbol -   A representation, one thing standing for another.

Type -   A prophetic representation, one thing prefiguring another.

Types are to be viewed as prophetic symbols. This is not to say that all symbols used in prophecy are types. For example, Daniel 7 is prophetic of Gentile kingdoms which are symbolized in this passage as "beasts". These beasts are not types (prophetic symbols, rather they are symbols used in prophecy). A type is prophetic in and of itself and does not

depend upon prophetic language for its prophetic import (e.g., Ge 22 provides us with a type having prophetic import without prophetic language).

A SYMBOL	A TYPE
May represent a thing, either past, present or future.	Is essentially a prefiguring of something future from itself.
Is a figure of something either past, present or future.	Is a figure of that which is to come.
Has in itself no essential reference to time.	Has inherent in itself a reference to time.
Is designed to represent certain characteristics or qualities in that which it represents.	Is designed to be a pre-ordained representation of something or someone to come.
To be interpreted, requires a pointing out of the characteristics, qualities, marks or features common to both the symbol and that which it symbolizes.	To be interpreted, generally requires a setting forth of an extended analogy between the type and that which it typifies.

The **ROCK** in Ps 18:2 is a symbol, not a type.
The **CANDLESTICKS** in Rev 1:20 are symbols, not types.
The **LAMB** in Jn 1:29 is a symbol, not a type.
The **RAINBOW** in Ge 9:13-16 is a symbol, not a type.
The **OLIVE TREES** in Zec 4:3 are symbols, not types.
The color **WHITE** in Rev 19:8 is a symbol, not a type.
The number **666** in Rev 13:18 is a symbol, not a type.

ADAM in Ro 5:14 is a type, not a symbol.
The offices of **PROPHET, PRIEST** and **KING** in 1Ki 1:34 are types, not symbols.
JONAH'S EXPERIENCE in the fish in Mt 12:39-41 is a type, not a symbol.

The whole of the animal system of sacrifice in Lev 1-5 is typical of Christ's sacrifice, yet the animals themselves are symbolic.

The Tabernacle of Moses in Ex 25-40 is a type, not a symbol. However, within the type there are numerous symbols.

It must be recognized, through this, that types involve symbols, but symbols of themselves are never types.

In Ex 12 the historical event of the Feast of Passover is a type of Christ and His Church. Within this type there are symbolic elements such as the lamb, the hyssop, the unleavened bread, and the bitter herbs, but these by themselves are not types.

In Ex 17 the historical event of the smiting of the rock is a type of the crucifixion of Christ. Within this type there are symbolic elements such as the rock and the rod, which by themselves are not types.

In all of the above there is an overlapping of type and symbol, symbol and type.

The above illustrations show the inter-relatedness of types and symbols to be such that while symbolism may be used in typology, the converse is never true.

IV.   CLASSIFICATION OF TYPES

God, knowing the end from the beginning, was able to cause the writing of the Old Testament to be done in such a way that many of its elements were meant to be viewed as anticipative of that which was to come in the New Testament. The types of the Old Testament may be divided into four main classifications: Persons, Offices, Institutions and Events.

A.   Typical Persons
        In the writing of Scripture, God caused the recording of history to be such that certain persons are meant to be viewed as prefiguring another person to come. These persons can be seen as foreshadowings in either their character, office, function or relationship to the history of redemption.

        Ro 5:12-21. Verse 14 - "Adam...who is the figure (Greek, "type") of Him that was to come..."

Here Paul, in setting forth an extended analogy shows Adam to be a type of Christ.

B.   Typical Offices
In writing Scripture, God meant for certain offices to be viewed as foreshadowings of offices to come.

Heb 5:1-10. Verses 4,5 - "...as was Aaron, so also Christ..."

The writer to the Hebrews here sets forth an extended analogy showing the Aaronic Priesthood to be typical of Christ's Priesthood.

C.   Typical Institutions
In writing Scripture, God means for certain institutions to be viewed as foreshadowings of institutions to come.

Heb 8:1-5. Verse 4 - "Who serve unto the example and shadow of heavenly things...the tabernacle..."

The writer to the Hebrews gives an extended analogy showing the instituting of the Mosaic Tabernacle to be typical of the heavenly institution.

D.   Typical Events
In the writing of Scripture, God caused historical events to be recorded in such a way that they may be viewed as foreshadowings of events to come.

1Co 10:1-11. Verse 6 - "Now these things were our examples (Greek: "types")..."

In this passage Paul refers to several historical events of Israel's wanderings in the wilderness as being typical of events in the experience of the New Testament Church.

NOTE: It should be recognized that these categories often overlap in Scripture. For instance: an event may include persons, offices and institutions.

These illustrations show that God, in authoring Scripture, was able to cause it to be written in such a way that many of the persons, offices, institutions and events were meant to be viewed as types of things to come.

Therefore, the literary method of prefiguring (typology) used in writing Scripture gives rise to the Typical Principle of interpreting Scripture.

V.   GUIDELINES FOR INTERPRETING THE TYPES

A.   The first step in using the Typical Principle is to correctly discern what elements, if any, of the passage under consideration are meant to be viewed as types.

B.   The use of this principle must be in constant conjunction with the context group of principles.

C.   Because types generally involve symbols, the Symbolic Principle must be constantly used in connection with the Typical Principle.

D.   The interpreter must ascertain the primary point of resemblance between the type and the antitype. Then he must realize the full correspondence between them by drawing out an extended analogy.

E.   The typical sense of Scripture is always solidly based on the literal or actual sense. Typical sense cannot be used to eradicate or contradict the actual sense.

1.   The significance of a type is based upon the literal nature and characteristics of that which is being used as a type.

2.   A type is meant to prefigure something essentially different from itself.

3.   The link between that which is used as a type and that which it typifies is the extended analogy that can be drawn between both.

F.   Generally speaking, the Bible interprets its own types, or at least gives the KEY to their interpretation. Thus the interpreter must search through the Scripture to discover the key by which he unlocks the door into the full interpretation of the type. The only safeguard against the human imagination's interpreting types is to let the Scripture interpret its own types. The best interpreter of Scripture is Scripture itself. To the honest searcher for truth there is hardly a type used in the Old Testament which is not interpreted or its key given in the New Testament. Many times just one verse of the New Testament is the key to the interpretation of many verses or chapters of that which is typical in the Old Testament.

e.g., Jn 1:14 becomes the key to interpreting the many chapters devoted to the Tabernacle of Moses in the Old Testament.

e.g., Jn 1:51 becomes the key to interpreting the chapter concerning Jacob's ladder in the Old Testament.

G.   There are types in the Old Testament that are neither interpreted nor have "keys" given in the New Testament. However, there are none of these that cannot be safely guided and governed in their interpretation by "example-types" that God gives us in Scripture.

Eph 5:22-33 implies that Adam and Eve are to be viewed as types of Christ and His bride. This becomes a sample-type by which we may interpret other Old Testament brides as types of the bride of Christ (Rebekah, Rachel, Ruth and Esther).

Heb 11:17-19, together with Jn 3:16 sets forth Abraham and Isaac as a type of the Father and Jesus in their Father/Son relationship. This becomes a sample-type by which we may interpret the relationship between Jacob and Joseph as a type.

H.   Often a type may have more than one application in its interpretation.

O.T. TYPE	INTERPRETATION	N.T. APPLICATIONS
Tabernacle of Moses	Point of Resemblance God's Dwelling Place	Christ - Jn 1:14 Church - Heb 3:1-5 Believer - Eph 3:17 Heaven's sanctuary - Heb 8:1-5

I.   The interpreter must recognize that a type is generally to be viewed as a prophecy. Many times God instructed His servants to do typically what He Himself would fulfill actually. For example, God the Father instructed Abraham to do typically that which He Himself planned to do actually (Ge 22). In another instance, God told Israel to do typically with the Passover lamb what He would fulfill actually with the True Lamb (Ex 12).

However, we must recognize that these were not types to those persons involved, but were actual circumstances, actual realities. Thus God takes the actual to be typical, which then becomes prophetical of another actual.

All types are to be viewed as God-ordained, not originating with man. Because all types are God-ordained, they hold an important place with Him (Notice Moses' punishment for spoiling a God-ordained type through his sin of disobedience. Ex 17 with Nu 20, and Ps 106:33; 1Co 10:1-4).

J.   No doctrines should be built on types alone, but types may be used to illustrate doctrines. However, their limitations must be recognized.

K.   No type is to be interpreted with another type, otherwise confusion results.

L.   The interpreter must recognize that there is no such thing as a "perfect type", for the very nature of things used as types were all stamped with imperfection and incompleteness. However, God used the imperfect and the incomplete as sign posts pointing to Christ, the Perfect and Complete One.

M.   The interpreter must be careful not to force the typological principle upon unsuitable passages. Some interpreters desiring to personalize Scripture, to establish eschatological truth, or even to point to Christ in the Old Testament have forced this principle upon passages to the point of distorting their interpretation.

Generally speaking, the nature and character of the person gives some indication as to whether such may be viewed as a type of Christ, or the antichrist, or saints or sinners.

N.   The interpreter should know also where a type begins and ends: e.g., Aaron is a type of Christ, especially in his office as high priest. He is certainly not a type of Christ when he sets up the golden calf worship. There is a beginning and ending where he is a type of Christ in his priesthood. This is true of other Bible characters and offices.

In conjunction with the Typical Principle, and Symbolic Principle, the Christocentric Principle needs to be used if the person typifies Christ in that which was Divinely wrought in his life.

VI.   ILLUSTRATION

In order to help the student to interpret types, following are some extended illustrations, using the Typical Principle.

A.   Typical Persons
Ge 37-50: These chapters cover the life story of Joseph. A consideration of his character and experiences leads us to view him as a type of Christ. The primary point of resemblance is to be seen in the Son's relationship to the Father.

O.T. Type	Point of Resemblance	Antitype
Joseph	Son's relation to Father	Jesus

In the extended analogy below only some of the most prominent correspondences are given. A full interpretation of this type would involve many more.

Joseph	Analogy	Jesus
Ge 30:22-24	A firstborn son	Mt 1:25
Ge 29:31	Miracle birth	Isa 7:14
Ge 37:2,3	Beloved son	Mt 3:16
Ge 37:2	A shepherd	Jn 10:11
Ge 35:22-26	Hated by half-brothers	Mk 3:31,32
Ge 37:5-10	Revelation of exaltation	Mt 26:64
Ge 37:12-14	Sent by father to brethren	Jn 5:24, 30, 43
Ge 37:18	Rejected by brethren	Jn 7:3
Ge 37:28	Sold for silver	Mt 27:3-10

Joseph	Analogy	Jesus
Ge 39:11-19	Falsely accused	Mk 14:55-60
Ge 40:1-4	Suffered as criminal	Lk 23:32
Ge 41:40,41	Exalted in due time	Ac 5:31
Ge 41:45	Given an exalted name	Php 2:9,10
Ge 41:43	All bow the knee	Php 2:10,11
Ge 41:45	Receives a Gentile bride	Eph 3:6
Ge 45:14,15	Brethren reconciled	Zec 12:10-14
Ge 47:1-7	Reunited with his father	Mk 16:19

B. Typical Offices
Ex 28: Heb 5:1-5; 8:1-4: These passages, together with many others, deal with the office of the High Priest. The qualifications and function of this office, as outlined under the Mosaic Covenant, support the fact that it is a type of Christ's own office under the New Covenant.

The primary point of resemblance is to be seen as Mediatorship.

O.T. Type	Point of Resemblance	Antitype
High Priest	Mediatorship	Christ's Priesthood

The following are only a few of the many correspondences within the extended analogy that can be drawn in the full interpretation of the type.

High Priest	Analogy	Christ's Priesthood
Nu 3:12	Born a priest	Zec 6:12,13
Ex 28:1	Taken from among men	Heb 2:17
Heb 5:4	Called of God	Heb 5:5
Ex 28:29,38	Ordained for men	Heb 5:5-10

High Priest	Analogy	Christ's Priesthood
Ex 28:41	Anointed for ministry	Jn 1:41
Lev 1:1-9	Offer sacrifice	Heb 8:3
Ex 28:1-4,41	Minister to God	Heb 7:22-26
Heb 5:2	Compassionate	Heb 2:17

C.   Typical Institutions

Ex 25-40: These chapters are devoted to the institution of the Tabernacle of Moses. The New Testament gives us the key (Jn 1:14) that enables us to interpret this institution as a type of Christ. The primary point of resemblance is to be seen in the fact that it is God's dwelling place.

O.T. Type	Point of Resemblance	Antitype
Tabernacle of Moses	God's Dwelling Place	Christ

The following are only a few of the many correspondences within the extended analogy that can be drawn in the full interpretation of this type.

Tabernacle of Moses	Analogy	Christ
Ark of the Covenant	"God with us"	Mt 1:23
The Mercy Seat	Propitiation	Ro 3:25
Rod that Budded	Resurrection	Jn 11:25
Golden Pot of Manna	Bread of Life	Jn 6:48-51
Tables of Law	Tables of Heart	Ps 40:8
The Name	Lord Jesus Christ	Ac 2:36
Altar of Incense	Intercessor	Heb 7:25
Golden Candlestick	Light of world	Jn 8:12
Table of Shewbread	Table of Lord	Mt 26:26-28

Tabernacle of Moses	Analogy	Christ
The Veil	His Flesh	Heb 10:20
The Door	The Door	Jn 10:9
The Gate	The Way	Jn 14:6
Brazen Altar	Blood Atonement	Heb 5:9-11
Brazen Laver	Cleansing	Eph 5:26

D.   Typical Events
Ge 6-9: These chapters provide us with the historical account of the event of the Flood. The circumstance and activity of this event is taken by Jesus to be typical of the Last Days.

The primary point of resemblance is judgment upon wickedness.

O.T. Type	Point of Resemblance	Antitype
The Flood	Judgment upon wickedness	Last Days

The following are only a few of the many correspondences within the extended analogy that can be drawn in the full interpretation of this type.

The Flood	Analogy	The Last Days
Ge 6:1	Population explosion	Lk 17:26,27
Ge 6:2	Intermarriage	"
Ge 6:5	Great wickedness	"
Ge 6:5	Evil thoughts and imaginations	"
Ge 6:11,12	Corruption	"
Ge 6:11,13	Violence	Mt 24:36-41; 2Pe 2:5

INTERPRETING THE SYMBOLS AND TYPES

The Flood	Analogy	The Last Days
Ge 6:8,9	Godly remnant	Mt 24:36-41; 2Pe 2:5
Ge 6:3; 1Pe 2:5	Spirit and Word at work	"
Heb 11:7	Ark of salvation	"
Ge 7:1-24	Judgment-Deluge	"
Ge 7:1-24	All wicked perish	"

CHAPTER THIRTEEN

THE CHRISTO-CENTRIC PRINCIPLE

I. DEFINITION

The Christo-Centric Principle is that principle by which Scripture is interpreted in relation to its center - Christ.

II. APPLICATION

The basis for this principle is the fact that Christ is the central person of the Bible. The entire written Word revolves around He who is the Living Word. His person and work is the theme of God's written revelation. In the wheel of divine revelation, He is the hub and all truths are as spokes relating to Him who is The Truth. The truth of this is best expressed in the following verses:

Heb 10:7   "...in the volume of the book it is written of *Me*..."

Jn 5:39   "Search the Scriptures...they are they which testify of *Me*."

Lk 24:27   "...He expounded unto them in all the Scriptures the things concerning *Himself*."

Lk 24:44   "...all things must be fulfilled which were written in the law of Moses; and in the prophets, and in the psalms, concerning *me*."

Ac 10:43   "To *Him* give all the prophets witness..."

Jn 1:45   "We have found *Him* of whom Moses in the law, and the prophets, did write."

NOTE ALSO: Jn 1:1,14; 5:46,47; Mt 5:17,18; Ac 3:18; Jn 14:6 with 17:17

All of these Scriptures attest to the fact that the Bible is Christ-centered; He is the living embodiment of the Written Word.

In that God is the author of Scripture He was able to center all of its subjects around the person and work of His Son: "that in all things *He* might have the pre-eminence" (Col 1:18). We will now illustrate this in each of the major divisions of Scripture:

The Old Testament Historical Books
The Old Testament Poetical Books
The Old Testament Prophetical Books
The Gospels
The Acts
The Epistles
The Apocalypse

There are many titles, symbols, and types of the Lord Jesus Christ in the total Bible. Following is a list of the most prominent and significant pictures and types of Christ in all the books of the Bible.

A. CHRIST IN THE OLD TESTAMENT HISTORICAL BOOKS

THE BOOK	OLD TESTAMENT	NEW TESTAMENT
Genesis		
The Creator	Ge 1, 2	Col 1:16
The Beginning	Ge 1, 2	Rev 1:8
The Seed of the Woman	Ge 3:15	Mt 1:23
The Ark of Salvation	Ge 6:18; 7:23	Lk 2:30
Isaac, the Only Begotten Son	Ge 22:1-19	Jn 3:16
Joseph, the Beloved Son	Ge 37:4	Mt 3:17
Exodus		
The Deliverer	Ex 3; 6:1-8	Ac 5:31
The Mediator	Ex 32:30-35;	Heb 8:6
	Ex 33:12-14	
The Lawgiver	Ex 20:1-12	Heb 8:10
The High Priest	Ex 28,29	Heb 2:17
Passover Lamb	Ex 12	1Co 5:7
Tabernacle of God with Man	Ex 40:34,35	Jn 1:14
Leviticus	Chapters	
Sacrifice and Oblation	Lev 1-7	Heb 10:12
Holy High Priest	Lev 8,9,10	Heb 7:26
The Atonement	Lev 16	Heb 9:14
Way of Approach to God	Lev 16	Heb 7:25

THE BOOK	OLD TESTAMENT	NEW TESTAMENT
Numbers		
The Tabernacle	Nu 3,4,9	Jn 1:14 (Grk Dwelt)
Sanctuary in Wilderness	Nu 3,4,7	Eze 11:16; Jn 1:14
The Nazarite	Nu 6	Heb 7:26
The Serpent of Brass	Nu 21:8,9	Jn 3:14
The Smitten Rock	Nu 20:8-13	1Co 10:4
The Star out of Jacob	Nu 24:17	Mt 2:2
Deuteronomy		
The True Prophet	Dt 18:15-19	Ac 3:22
The Rock	Dt 32:4,18,31	1Co 10:4
Joshua		
Joshua (Jehoshua)	Jos 1-24	Heb 4:8
Captain of our Salvation	Jos 5:13-15	Heb 2:10
The Man with the Sword	Jos 5:13-15	Eph 6:12-18
Inheritance Giver	Jos 13-19	Heb 4; Eph 1:3,14
Judges		
Judge/Deliverer/Savior	Jdg 2:13-23	Mt 1:21-23
Anointed by Spirit of Lord	Jdg 13	Jn 1:41-42 (Christ)
Ruth		
The Mighty Man	Ru 2:1	Lk 1:49
Lord of the Harvest	Ru 2:14-17	Lk 10:1-2
Kinsman Redeemer	Ru 4:1-12	Rev 5:9,10
1 Samuel		
Anointed Prophet/		Lk 1:31-35;
Priest/King/Intercessor	1Sa 16:1,13	Matt 27:37
2 Samuel		
Son of David	2Sa 7	Mt 1:1
1 Kings		
King of Peace and Glory	1Ki 1,2,3,4	Mt 1:1
The Wisdom of God	1Ki 3:4-9	1Co 1:30
Temple Builder	1Ki 5,6,7,8	Eph 2:20-22
Greater than Solomon	1Ki 10	Mt 12:42
The Prophet/God's Word	1Ki 13:1-3	Jn 1:14
King of Kings/Lord of Lords	1Ki 22:19	Rev 19:16
2 Kings		
The Righteous King	2Ki 3:12	1Co 1:30
The Man of God	2Ki 1:12	Lk 23:47
Word of the Lord in Person	2Ki 3:12	Jn 1:14

THE BOOK	OLD TESTAMENT	NEW TESTAMENT
1 Chronicles The Greater King David	 1Ch 11:1-3	Mt 1:1 Rev 22:16
2 Chronicles Prophet/Priest/King Temple Cleanser Reformer	 2Ch 20:14-21 2Ch 1:11,12; 7:29 2Ch 29:1-19	Heb 9:11; 2:17 Rev 19:16 Mt 21:12,13 Heb 9:10
Ezra Governor/Priest Scribe and Restorer	Ezr 6:7 Ezr 10:10 Ezr 6:2-7	Heb 5:1-5 Mt 2:6 Isa 58:12 with Acts 3:20-21
Nehemiah Governor of Judah Man of Prayer and Work	Ne 5:14 Ne 2:4-8 Ne 3:1-10	Mt 2:6 Jn 17 Mt 16:18
Esther Great King and His Bride	Est 1:1-8 Est 2:17	 Rev 19:7

B. CHRIST IN THE OLD TESTAMENT POETICAL BOOKS

THE BOOK	OLD TESTAMENT	NEW TESTAMENT
Job Patient Suffering Priest	Job 1:20-22; 40:8,10	Heb 5:1-5
Psalms Beloved Shepherd/King The Sweet Singer/Worshipper	Ps 23 Ps 139-145	Jn 3:16; 10:11,14 Heb 2:12
Proverbs The Wisdom of God	Pr 1,2	1Co 1:20, 24; Col 2:3
Ecclesiastes The Preacher in Jerusalem The Son of David The Wisdom of God The King "from above"	Ecc 1:1 Ecc 1:1	Lk 4:18-20 Mt 1:1 1Co 1:30 Gal 4:26
Son of Solomon King of Peace/Bridegroom lover	SS 1-8	Jn 14:27; Eph 5:23-32

THE BOOK	OLD TESTAMENT	NEW TESTAMENT
Habakkuk Judge of Babylon The Rewarder of Faith	Hab 1:5-11 Hab 2:1-4	Rev 17,18 Heb 10:38; 11:6
Zephaniah The Jealous God and Executor of God's Wrath	Zep 1:18	2Co 11:2; Ro 2:5,6
Haggai Prophet/Priest/Prince and builder of the Lord's House	Hag 1,2,3	Mt 16:18; Heb 1:1,2; Heb 3:1-4
Zechariah Whom Jehovah Remembers The Branch Jehovah's Servant The Smitten Shepherd King-Priest/Temple Builder King over all the earth	Name Interpreted Zec 3:8 Zec 3:8 Zec 13:7 Zec 6:9-12 Zec 14:9	 Mt 2:23 Php 2:7-9 Mk 14:27 Heb 5:5,6; Eph 2:20-22 Rev 19:16
Malachi Messenger of Covenant, Refiner/Purifier/Cleanser of the Temple	Mal 3:1-3	Mt 3:11; Jn 2:13-17 Mt 21:12-14; 26:26-28

C. CHRIST IN THE OLD TESTAMENT PROPHETICAL BOOKS

THE BOOK	OLD TESTAMENT	NEW TESTAMENT
Isaiah The Holy One of Israel Our Salvation Our Righteousness Our Comfort The True Judge	Isa 30:11,12,15,29 Isa 12 Isa 51:4-8 Isa 51:3; 66:13 Isa 2:4	Mk 1:24 Mt 1:21 1Co 1:30 Jn 14:16,18 Jn 5:22
Jeremiah The Appointed Prophet The Righteous Branch/King The Lord our Righteousness	Jer 1:5 Jer 23:5 Jer 23:4-6	Ac 3:22-24 1Co 1:30 1Co 1:30

THE BOOK	OLD TESTAMENT	NEW TESTAMENT
Lamentations The Weeping Prophet The Man of Sorrows	La 1:16 La 1:12,18	Lk 19:41-44 Mt 23:37,38
Ezekiel The Son of Man The Shekinah Glory	Eze 2:1-8; 3:1-4 Eze 43:1-4	Jn 1:51 Jn 1:14-18
Daniel The Son of Man The Crushing Stone The Kingdom of God in person King of Kings/Lord of Lords	Da 7:13 Da 2:34-35 Da 7:27 Da 7:27	Jn 1:51 Mt 21:42-44 Ro 14:17 Rev 19:16
Hosea Prophet of Law and Love	Hos 1,2	Ac 3:22,23; Mt 5:17,18; Jn 3:16
Joel Jehovah-God, Promiser and Baptizer in the Holy Spirit	Joel 2:28-32	Lk 24:49; Ac 2:33 Jn 1:31-33
Amos Burden bearer and the Judge/Punisher of nations Builder of David's Tabernacle	Am 1 Am 9:11-15	2Th 1:7-9 Mt 16:18,19; Ac 15:15-18
Obadiah Servant/Worshipper and Executor of Divine Wrath	Ob 15,17,21	Heb 2:12; 2Th 1:6-10
Jonah The Greater than Jonah	Jnh 1:17	Mt 12:39-41
Micah Heavenly Micah, "Like God" Rejected King of the Jews Establisher of His house	Mic 7:17,18 Mic 5:1 Mic 4:1,2	Heb 1:2-4 Jn 19:15 Heb 3:6
Nahum Prophet of Comfort and Vengeance	Na 1:2-7,15; 2:2	Jn 14:16; 2Th 1-8

D. CHRIST IN THE GOSPELS

THE BOOK	SCRIPTURE REFERENCES
Matthew King/Lawgiver Anointed, Son of David Fulfiller of Law and Prophets	Mt 2:2; Mt 5,6,7 Mt 1:1; 3:16,17 Mt 5:17; 11:13
Mark Son of Man/Son of God Suffering Servant who became Lord	Mk 10:45 Mk 16:19
Luke Son of Man, Anointed, Preacher and Savior	Lk 4:18, 19; 19:10
John The Word, the Eternal Son The Life and the Light The "I AM" The Way, the Truth, the Life	Jn 1:1; 3:16 Jn 1:4,5 Jn 8:56 Jn 14:6

E. CHRIST IN THE ACTS

THE BOOK	SCRIPTURE REFERENCES
Acts Christ, Head of the Church, Baptizer in the Holy Spirit	Ac 1:5-8 Ac 2:1-4

F. CHRIST IN THE EPISTLES

THE BOOK	SCRIPTURE REFERENCES
Romans Salvation/Righteousness of God The Propitiation/Mercy Seat	Ro 10:3,4 Ro 3:25 (Greek)
1 Corinthians Power and Wisdom of God Righteousness, Sanctification Wisdom and Redemption The Love of God Resurrection and the Life	1Co 1:30 1Co 1:30-31 1Co 1:24-30 1Co 13 1Co 15

THE BOOK	SCRIPTURE REFERENCES
2 Corinthians Comforter/Apostle and Sin Offering Glory of the New Covenant	2Co 5:21 2Co 3,4
Galatians Faith, Righteousness, Seed of Abraham, New Covenant Mediator	Gal 3
Ephesians Fullness of God Head of the Church The Bridegroom Giver of Ministries Grace and Peace of God	Eph 4:9-16 Eph 4:15 Eph 5:22-32 Eph 4:9-16 Eph 1:2,3
Philippians Our Joy, Life, Mind, Goal and Strength	Php 2,3,4
Colossians The Pre-existent, Pre-eminent One, Creator, Ruler, Redeemer, Head of the Body, Fullness of Godhead Bodily	Col 1:19; 2:9
1 Thessalonians Our Sanctification, and our Coming Lord	1Th 5:23,2
2 Thessalonians The Avenger and Coming Lord	2Th 1:6-10
1 Timothy Elder/Deacon/Teacher who fulfills His Divine Charge	1Ti 3
2 Timothy Savior/Seed of David/Righteous Judge/Lord of the Heavenly Kingdom	2Ti 4:1
Titus Savior/Grace of God and Redeemer	Tit 1:3; 2:10-14
Philemon Intercessor/Advocate	Whole Epistle of Paul's heart
Hebrews Angel of God/Prophet/High Priest/ Minister/Sacrifice/Author and Finisher of Faith	Heb 1-13

THE BOOK	SCRIPTURE REFERENCES
James Lord of Glory The Judge The Lord of Hosts The Husbandman	 Jas 2:1 Jas 4:11,12 Jas 5:4 Jas 5:7
1 Peter The Foreordained Lamb The Chief Cornerstone Stone of Stumbling/Rock of Offence The Example/Chief Shepherd and Bishop	 1Pe 1:19-20 1Pe 2:6 1Pe 2:8 1Pe 5:1-4
2 Peter The Beloved Son The Dayspring and Coming Lord	 2Pe 1:17 2Pe 1:19; 3:10
1 John The Word/the Son/Advocate and Propitiation/Christ who is Love, Light and Life	 1Jn 1,2,3,4
2 John The Truth/the Son of God/the Christ	 2Jn
3 John The Truth	 3Jn 4,8
Jude The Coming Lord, Judge and Only Wise God, our Savior	 Jude 14,25

G. CHRIST IN THE APOCALYPSE

THE BOOK	SCRIPTURE REFERENCES
Revelation Head of the Church The Lamb of God The Lion of the Tribe of Judah The Jehovah Angel/Messenger The Bridegroom The Word, King of Kings and Lord of Lords	 Rev 1,2,3 Rev 5:5; 14:1-2 Rev 5:5 Rev 7:1-3; 10:1-5 (implied) Rev 19:5-8 Rev 19:11-16

(Note: This chapter is taken from **Interpreting the Scriptures** by Conner/Malmin)

105

Christ is indeed the hub of Biblical revelation. "In the volume of the book it is written of Me," Jesus said (Ps 40:7 with Heb 10:7).

The student is referred to the guidelines for interpreting the types properly so as not to force the Christo-centric Principle beyond its Biblically defined limits.

CHAPTER FOURTEEN

TYPICAL PERSONS

In briefly listing the following persons, who may be viewed in a typical manner, it should be remembered that there is no such thing as "a perfect type". The very nature of man is stamped with imperfection. All persons mentioned in the Bible can certainly be studied as character studies from which all can learn either what to do or what not to do.

However, God undoubtedly set forth some real historical people who are certainly seen, by analogy, to be types of Christ or the Antichrist, or the Church, both true and false.

In the following list, we group those persons in Scripture who may be viewed as types of Christ, types of Antichrist, or types of the church, both the true church and the false church. Some of these are specifically seen in Scripture and others are implied, their very nature and character setting such forth.

Specific Scriptures are given from the Old Testament and corresponding suitable references are given from the New Testament, where possible. The student is referred to the guidelines and safeguards for interpreting types in Scripture, whether specific or implied.

I.   TYPES OF CHRIST

TYPE	INTERPRETATION	O.T. SCRIPTURE	N.T. SCRIPTURE
Aaron	High priest	Ex 28:1-4	Heb 5:4-6
Abel	Shepherd/martyr	Ge 4:1-8	Heb 12:24
Abraham	Father of all who believe	Ge 15:6	Ro 4:11
Adam	Head of Creation	Ge 5:2	Ro 5:14; 1Co 15:45
Boaz	Kinsman-redeemer	Ru 2,3,4	Rev 5:9-10

TYPE	INTERPRETATION	O.T. SCRIPTURE	N.T. SCRIPTURE
Daniel	Prophet/Seer of world kingdoms	Da 1-7	Rev 19:16; 11:15
David	King, prophet, Psalmist, worshipper	2Sa 23:1-2	Heb 2:12; Ac 2:25-36
Eliezer	The Servant one	Ge 15:2; 24:2	Mt 12:17-18
Enoch	Translated one	Ge 5:24	Heb 11:5
Ezra	Scribe, Priest, Hermeneutician	Ezr 10	Lk 24:27; Heb 5:1-5
Isaac	Only begotten son	Ge 22	Heb 11:17-19
Job	The Suffering saint	Job 1,2	Jas 5:10-11
Jonah	The Sign-prophet	Jnh 1,2,3	Mt 12:40-41
Joseph	The beloved son	Ge 37:1-3	Heb 11:22
Joshua	Captain of Lord's Host	Jos 5:12-15	Heb 2:10
Judah	Lion tribe, Kingly seed	Ge 49:9	Rev 5:5; Heb 7:14
Melchizedek	King Priest with eternal oath	Ge 14:18-20; Ps 110	Heb 7
Moses	Prophet, Priest, Lawgiver	Ex 20:1; Dt 18:15-18	Jn 1:17
Nehemiah	Governor, Rebuilder of city walls	Ne 4:18	Mt 2:5-6
Noah	Ark of safety-builder, rest in storms	Ge 6,7,8	1Pe 3:20-21; Heb 11:7
Phinehas	Everlasting Priesthood	Nu 25:11	Heb 7
Samson	Mighty/Deliverer Judge	Jdg 11,12,13	Jn 1:42; 1Pe 2:4-8
Samuel	Judge-Prophet	1Sa 3:20-21; Jer 15:1	Ac 3:24-26

TYPE	INTERPRETATION	O.T. SCRIPTURE	N.T. SCRIPTURE
Solomon	King of Peace, Temple builder	1Ki 1-8	Mt 16:15-20; Eph 2:19-22
Zadok	Priesthood	Eze 44:15-18	Heb 5,6,7
Zerubbabel	Governor, Temple foundation layer	Zec 4:8-10	1Co 5:9-16

II.   TYPES OF CHRIST AND HIS BRIDE

Paul is the one who provides probably the only specific picture of the marriage of Christ and His bride, the church. In Eph 5:23-32, he weaves together both the natural relationship of the man and the woman, the husband and the wife, and then woven throughout is the "great mystery" of the marriage of Christ and His church.

Paul actually goes back to the very original marriage of Adam and Eve and uses the very words out of the mouth of Adam and applies them also to the marriage of Christ to His bride. This gives us some guidelines and foundation for the use of the typical principle in relation to other brides that are not specifically mentioned as such, but are such, by implication.

The other apostle who would provide a picture of the bride of Christ was the apostle John.   This he did in Rev 21-22. There the church is seen as "the bride city". She is adorned as a bride to meet her husband.

The "sample-type" of Adam and Eve, as used by Paul, provides enough guidelines for the student to consider other men and women as types of Christ and His bride. For these we list the Old Testament Scriptures. These need to be studied in their particular life stories in order to do an extended analogy.

TYPE	INTERPRETATION	SCRIPTURES
Adam/Eve	Christ and His Bride Sinless Marriage	Ge 1:26-28; 2:18-25; Jn 3:27; Eph 5:23-32; Rev 21:3
Abraham/Sarah	God and Israel	Jer 3:6-14; Eze 16:8-14
Isaac/Rebekah	Christ and His Church	Ge 24
Jacob/Rachel	Christ and His Church	Ge 29
Joseph/Asenath	Christ and His Bride	Ge 41:45
Moses/Zipporah	Christ and His Bride	Ex 2:21
High Priest/Bride	Christ and His Bride	Lev 21:10-13
Salmon/Rahab	Christ and His Bride	Jos 2:1
Boaz/Ruth	Christ and His Bride	Ru 4:13-15
Solomon/Shulamite	Christ and His Church	SS 5
Ahasuerus/Esther	Christ and His Church	Est 2:16,17

III. TYPES OF THE CHURCH

A woman in Scripture is used as a type of a church, whether the true or false church. Some godly women are noted who may be viewed as types of the true church, the bride of Christ. Some ungodly women are noted who may be viewed as types of the false or harlot church.

A. The Bride of Christ

1. Hebrew Brides

BRIDE	SCRIPTURE
Sarah	Ge 17
Rebekah	Ge 24
Rachel	Ge 29

2.   Gentile Brides

BRIDE	SCRIPTURE
Asenath	Ge 41:45
Zipporah	Ex 2:21
Rahab	Jos 2:1; Mt 1:5
Ruth	Ru 4:13-15; Mt 1:5
Queen of Sheba	2Ch 9:1-12; Mt 12:42
Woman and Coin - Espousal to Christ	Lk 15:8-10 with 2Co 11:1-3

All the above point to the church, the bride of Christ, which will be composed of believing Jews and Gentiles, who become one in Christ at the cross (Eph 2:11-22; 1Co 12:13).

B.   The Harlot Church

TYPE	INTERPRETATION	SCRIPTURE
Jezebel	The Murderous Church	1Ki 16:31; 21:25; Rev 2:20
Woman and Leaven	The Corrupting Church	Mt 13:33
Goddess Diana	The Idolatrous Church	Ac 19:24-28
Great Whore	The Harlot Church	Rev 17:1-5

The character of these evil women shadow forth different aspects of the great harlot church.

IV.   TYPICAL PERSONS - NAMED

There are other persons named in Scripture who may be viewed as types of the antichrist and/or unregenerate persons. All become great character studies as well as typical persons of prophetic import.

TYPE	INTERPRETATION	O.T. SCRIPTURES	N.T. SCRIPTURES
Absalom	The rebel son	2Sa 14:25	
Achan	The accursed one	Jos 7:1-15	
Adonijah	The usurper king	1Ki 1:5-10	
Agag	The destroyer king	1Sa 15:9	
Amalek	The hater of Israel	Ge 36:12	
Balaam	The licentious prophet	Nu 22,23	Rev 2:14; 2Pe 2:15; Jude 11
Cain	The lamb rejector and murderer	Ge 4:5	Heb 11:4; Jude 11; 1Jn 3:12
Canaanites	Principalities, and powers, wicked spirits	Ex 3:8	Eph 6:11,12
Esau	Seed of the flesh	Ge 25:24-34	Ro 9:10-13
Goliath	Defier of Israel	1Sa 17	
Ishmael	Seed of the flesh Law Covenant	Ge 16	Gal 4:22-31
Judas	Son of perdition, Fallen apostle		Jn 17:12; Ac 1:25
Saul	The apostate king	1Ch 10:13,14	2Th 2:1-12

V.   TYPICAL PERSONS - PATRIARCHS

The earliest patriarchs are seen shadowing forth certain truths pertaining to the Father God, the Son of God or His apostles.

TYPE	INTERPRETATION	SCRIPTURES
Adam	The First and Last Man	Ge 1:26-28; 5:1-2; Ro 5:11-21
Abraham	The Everlasting Father	Ge 17:1-5; Isa 9:6-9
Isaac	The only begotten Son	Ge 22; Heb 11:17-19

TYPE	INTERPRETATION	SCRIPTURES
Jacob	The Anointer of Bethel	Ge 28:17-22; 2Cor 1:21,22
Joseph	Rejected, beloved Son	Ge 37; Ac 7:8-13
Judah	The Sceptred One	Ge 49:10; Rev 5:5
Noah	The Rest bringer by the Ark of Safety	Ge 7,8; Lk 17:26-27; 2Pe 2:5
Reuben	Fallen son of the twelve	Ge 49:3,4 with Ac 1:25
Twelve sons of Jacob	The twelve apostles	Ge 49; Lk 9:1-2

VI.   TYPICAL PERSONS - UNNAMED

TYPE	INTERPRETATION	SCRIPTURES
Babe	New convert	Heb 5:12; 1Pe 2:2
Children	Young convert, immature	1Jn 2:12-14
Daughter of Zion	Local church, from a mother church	Isa 1:8; 4:3-6; Heb 12:22-24
Daysman(Umpire)	Christ our Mediator	Job 9:32,33; 1Ti 2:5
Father	Spirituality, fatherhood	1Co 4:15
Hireling, Thief, Robber	False ministries of Satan, covetous for money	Jn 10:1,10-13
Leper	Sinful state of man	Lev 13,14; Mt 8:1-4
One hung on a tree	An accursed one	Dt 21:23; Gal 3:13
Virgin	Purity, New Covenant church	2Co 11:2,3
Whore/Harlot	Backslider, apostate	Jer 3:6-11, 14; Jas 4:4; Rev 17:1-5
Wife/woman	Old Testament wife of Jehovah, Israel	Jer 6:2; 31:31-34
Widow	Divorced, profane Israel	La 1:1; Jer 3:6-14

CHAPTER FIFTEEN

TYPICAL OFFICES

Certain offices were set forth by the Lord also to typify the offices that Christ Himself would fulfill. The function of these men pointed prophetically to the function that Jesus would fulfill. The historical became typical and prophetical.

It is worthy to note that God buried His workman but He continued on His work! He buried the man but He did not bury the ministry, or the office. In other words, God buried men who held the office of prophet, priest, judge or king, or even apostle, prophet, evangelist, shepherd and teacher, etc., but He continues the ministry on in Christ and His ministers.

Following is a list of the most prominent ministries, offices or functions, all of which are fulfilled perfectly in the Lord Jesus Christ Himself, of whom all others were but imperfect types and shadows.

Again, Old Testament and New Testament Scriptures are provided, as appropriate, whether specified or implied. It is the office that pointed to Christ, not necessarily the character of those who held office, because of their human frailties and imperfections.

TYPICAL OFFICES OF CHRIST

THE OFFICE	INTERPRETATION	O.T. SCRIPTURES	N.T. SCRIPTURES
Angel of the Lord	Christ as the Messenger of God	Jdg 13:15-22	Jn 1:1-3,14-18
Apostle	Christ the Sent One		Heb 3:1; Jn 5:23
Avenger of blood	Christ the Avenger	Nu 35:16-34	Rev 6:10; 11:18
Bishop/Elder	Christ the Overseer		1Pe 2:25; Heb 13:20
Deacon	Christ the Servant		Mk 10:42-45

THE OFFICE	INTERPRETATION	O.T. SCRIPTURES	N.T. SCRIPTURES
Evangelist	Christ the Good Tidings	Isa 61:1-3	Lk 4:16-19
Judge	Christ the Judge and Deliverer	Jdg 2:16-18	Jn 5:22
King	Christ the King and Lawgiver	Isa 33:22; Jer 23:1-5	Mt 2:2-6; Rev 19:16
Kinsman Redeemer	Christ our Redeemer and Kinsman by virgin birth	Jer 32:6-12	Rev 5:9-10
Messenger of the Covenant	Christ the New Covenant personified	Mal 3:1-13	Mt 26:26-28
Priest	Christ our Mediator and Intercessor		Heb 3:1; 5:1-5; 1Ti 2:5
Prophets	Christ the WORD of God, God's Spokesman		Jn 1:1-3,14-18; 1Jn 5:7; Heb 1:1-2
Schoolmaster	The Law our Guardian		Gal 3:24,25
Shepherd	Christ our Shepherd, lays down His life	Isa 40:11; Ps 23:1	Jn 10:1-5; Heb 13:20
Teacher	Christ the Revelation of God		Jn 3:2
Watchman	Christ our Guard and Watcher of souls	Eze 3:17	Heb 13:7,17,20

All ministries, graces, gifts, offices and functions find their full and complete expression in Christ. All such flow from the risen head now into the many-membered Body of Christ on earth, which is the church (1Co 12; Jn 1:14-18; Ro 12:1-8; Eph 4:9-16).

His graces, His gifts, His ministries, His offices and functions are not in any one person. All are to be found in the "one new man", the many members of the church, which is His Body, the fullness of Him who fills all in all (Eph 1:21-23).

CHAPTER SIXTEEN

TYPICAL INSTITUTIONS

God also used certain institutions in Israel as foreshadowings of Christ and His Church. These institutions were historical/material structures in Israel, but within them were both symbolical and typical elements. They pointed to Christ and to the Body of Christ, His Church.

The three main institutions are briefly listed here.

I.   THE TABERNACLE OF MOSES
The whole of the institution of the Tabernacle of Moses was prophetic of Christ. "The WORD was made flesh and dwelt (Grk Lit "tabernacled, pitched His tent) among us, and we beheld His glory..." (Jn 1:14-18).

The whole of the services of the priesthood, the sacrificial system, the festival occasions and the Tabernacle services pointed to the ministry of Christ in both the heavenly sanctuary, and His earthly sanctuary, the Church.

The Book of Hebrews, chapter after chapter, confirms these things. The student is referred to the Bibliography.

II.   THE TABERNACLE OF DAVID
The whole of the institution of the Tabernacle of David was also prophetic of Christ and His ministry both in heaven and in the Church. The Davidic order of worship shadowed forth the order of worship in the New Testament Church, after the sacrifice of Christ on the cross. Jew and Gentile come together to worship as one within the rent veil in the true Tabernacle of David (Am 9:11-15; Ac 15:15-18 with Heb 12). The student is referred to the Bibliography.

III.   THE TEMPLE OF SOLOMON
The same is true of the final habitation of God in the Old Testament, the Temple of the Lord, known as Solomon's Temple. All that was involved in the Tabernacle of Moses and the Tabernacle of David was incorporated into the Temple order.

The Temple becomes prophetic, symbolical and typical of Christ who is THE Temple of God and the Church, which is also God's Temple. It also shadowed on earth the heavenly Temple, as a number of Scriptures clearly speak (Rev 15; Rev 11:19; Rev 21-22; Heb 9-10). Again, the student is referred to the Bibliography.

The text-books recommended in the Bibliography deal fully with the typical, prophetical import of these institutions, as well as all of the symbols therein.

CHAPTER SEVENTEEN

TYPICAL EVENTS

As seen already, the Lord also used many historical and actual events to become typical and prophetical of events pertaining to the Messiah's times. The following are some of the most important historical/actual events, with their interpretation and application for Christians under New Covenant realities.

THE EVENT	INTERPRETATION	O.T. SCRIPTURES	N.T. SCRIPTURES
Blood on door posts, lintels	Faith application of redemption	Ex 12:12,13	Heb 11:28
Bruising of serpent's head	Satan's head crushed	Ge 3:15	Ro 16:20
Bruising of the heel	Christ crucified	Ge 3:15	Ro 16:20; Mt 26
Conquering Canaan land	Possess our inheritance	Jos 11:23	Ac 26:18; 1Pe 1:4
Cleansing of leper	Cleansing of sinner	Lev 13,14	Mt 8:1-4
Consecration of priests, blood, water, oil	Consecration of the believer	Ex 28,29	1Jn 5:8; Rev 1:6
Exodus from Egypt	Depart from bondage of sin and Satan	Ex 12,13	1Co 10:1,2; Jude 5
Isaac's sacrifice	Sacrifice of Christ by His Father	Ge 22	Heb 11:17-19; Jn 3:16
Jordan crossing	Entrance to inheritance	Jos 3,4	Heb 3:8,9
Lightnings and thunderings, voices	Activity of God's throne	Ex 19,20	Rev 4:5; 8:5
Lot's Days	Judgment by fire	Ge 19	Lk 17:28-30

THE EVENT	INTERPRETATION	O.T. SCRIPTURES	N.T. SCRIPTURES
Manna gathered	Feeding on Bread of Life	Ex 16	Jn 6
Marriage of the Lamb	Union of Christ and His bride, the church		Jn 3:29; Rev 19:6-9
Noah's Days	Judgment by water	Ge 6,7,8	Lk 17:26,27
Passover	Christ the Lamb of God	Ex 12	1Co 5:6-8
Pentecost	The Holy Spirit in the Church	Lev 23:15-17	Ac 2:1-4
Red Sea crossed	Separation from world by water baptism	Ex 13,14	1Co 10:1,2
Sabbaths	Kingdom Rest	Ge 2:1-3	Heb 4:9
Seasons, four	Cycle of Nature and dealings of God	Ecc 3:1; Ge 1:14; Pr 6:8	Gal 6:9; 1Th 5:1
Serpent of brass on pole	Christ lifted up as sin for us	Nu 21:1-9	Jn 3:14-16
Tabernacles Feast	Fullness of harvest blessing	Lev 23:23-44	Jas 5:7,8
Temple of Solomon	Christ and His Church	2Ch 5	Jn 2:20,21; 1Co 3:16
Three days and nights	Sign of cross; death, burial, resurrection of Christ	Jnh 1:17	Mt 12:39,40
Veil of the Temple, rent	End of Old Testament dispensation; access to God's throne	Ex 26:31,32	Mt 27:51; Heb 9:6-10; 10:19,20

THE EVENT	INTERPRETATION	O.T. SCRIPTURES	N.T. SCRIPTURES
Waters from smitten rock by the rod	Christ smitten of the Father on Calvary, and waters of the Holy Spirit flowing	Ex 17	1Co 10:1-4
Waters of Separation	Washing of water by the Word	Nu 19	Heb 9:13,14; Eph 5:26,27
Wilderness Wanderings	Failure and unbelief to enter inheritance	Nu 13,14	Heb 3,4; Jude 5

CHAPTER EIGHTEEN

ALPHABETICAL LISTING OF SYMBOLS AND TYPES

Following is a list of the Symbols and Types in this text arranged in alphabetical order.

Much of the text in this book is in a three column approach and has its limitations. In this alphabetical listing, additional Scriptures have been added as well as some other thoughts as appropriate.

The student should remember that, sometimes the interpretation is clearly specified and other times implied. The author has endeavored to provide Scriptures that are clear as possible, while some are implicit. However, when such are compared in the light of total Scripture, the interpretation and application can be seen. This then becomes a good base for an extended analogy of the Symbols and Types.

SYMBOLS AND TYPES

AARON
Type of Christ as High Priest. "Enlightened, Mountaineer, Lofty." Ex 28:1-8; Lev 21:10; Heb 3:1; 5:1-2; 9:7,24,25.

ABEL
Type of Christ as Shepherd. "Breath, vapor, mourning, transitory." Ge 4:2-10; Mt 23:35; Heb 12:24; 1Jn 3:12-13.

ABRAHAM
Type of God the Father. "Father of a great multitude." Ge 22:1-10; Heb 11:17-19; Jn 3:16.

ADAM
Type of Headship of Christ, the Last Adam. "Red earth, ruddy, earthy." Ge 2:19-20; 1Co 15:45-47; Ro 5:11-21.

ADDER — Symbol of Satan, viper, serpent, and false teachers. Ps 140:3; Ge 49:17; Ps 58:4; Pr 25:32.

ADULTERY — Symbol of violation of marriage vows. Eze 23:45; Jas 4:4. Spiritual idolatry.

ALABASTER BOX — Symbol of fragrance of Christ's brokenness and sacrifice. Perfume vase. "White stone." Mk 14:3; Mt 26:7; Lk 7:37.

ALGUM — Symbol of Christ's humanity. Red sandalwood, temple timber. 2Ch 2:8; 9:10-11; 1Ki 10:11-12.

ALMOND — Symbol of Christ in resurrection. "Hastening tree, Wakeful." The first tree to awake from winter sleep. Ex 25:33-34; Nu 17:8; Jer 1:11 with 1Co 15:20-23.

ALOES — Symbol of fragrance. Ps 45:8; Pr 7:17; SS 4:14; Jn 19:39.

ALTAR — Symbol of place of slaughter, sacrifice, death, or incense. Altars of earth, stone, brass, gold. Ge 8:20; 12:7; Ex 20:24-26; 2Ki 11:18; 18:22; Rev 8:3; Ex 30:1-10. Means "high, lifted up."

AMBER — Symbol of the Presence and Glory of God in judgment. Eze 1:4,27; 8:2.

AMETHYST — Symbol of royal priesthood. The 12 stones in High Priest's breastplate. Ex 28:19; 39:12; Rev 21:20.

ANCHOR — Symbol of safety, security, hope. "Hook." Heb 6:18-19; Ac 27:29,30,40.

ANOINT

Symbol of sanctification, set apart for service. "To rub with oil, to smear on." Ex 28:41; 30:26; Jdg 9:15; 1Sa 15:1; 1Jn 2:20,27.

ANT

Symbol of diligence, industry, wisdom in preparation. Pr 30:25; 6:6

APPAREL

Symbol of man's covering. Isa 63:1-3; Rev 19:7-8.

APPLE

Symbol of fragrance, beauty, sweetness. "Fragrance." Dt 32:10; Pr 25:11; Joel 1:12; SS 2:3; 7:8.

ARK
(Noah's)

Symbol of Christ our Safety and Salvation. Ge 7:7-9; 6:14; Mt 24:39; 1Pe 3:18-22.

ARK
(Covenant)

Symbol of Christ in humanity and deity; throne and presence of God among His people. The Mediator. "A chest, box, coffin." Ex 25:10-16; 1Ti 2:5; Php 2:9-11; Heb 1:3; 10:12; 12:24.

ARM
(of Lord)

Symbol of God's power. Help, mightiness, strength. Ex 15:16; 2Ki 17:36; Ps 89:10; 10:15; Isa 53:1.

ARMIES
(Horses, horsemen or locusts)

Symbol of spiritual powers and strength, good or evil. Rev 19:14-19; Joel 1:4; Rev 9:1-13; Zec 6:1-8.

ARMOR

Symbol of Divine equipment for warfare. Eph 6:10-18; Ro 13:12.

ARROW

Symbol of swift, silent judgments. "A piercer." Ps 18:14; Job 6:4; 2Ki 13:14-19; Job 38:2.

ASLEEP

Symbol of rest, refreshment or spiritual stupor, indifference. Ac 7:60; 1Co 15:6,7; Isa 52:11; Ro 13:11; Eph 5:14.

ASHES	Symbol of complete destruction, desolation, mourning, sorrow. "Consumed." Eze 28:18; 2Pe 2:6; Job 2:8; 42:6; Isa 58:5; Mal 4:3; Mt 11:21.
ASP	Symbol of false teachers, Satan's hosts. Adder. Job 20:11-16; Dt 32:33; Ro 3:13.
ASS (Donkey)	Symbol of patience, endurance, fortitude, strength, or stubbornness. Zec 9:9; Mt 21:3-7; Da 5:21; Ge 49:14. Burden-bearer.
ATONEMENT (by blood)	Symbol of redemption, appeasement of God's wrath, Calvary. Lev 17:11-14; Rev 5:9-10.
AWAKE	Symbol of alertness, watchfulness. Isa 52:1; 1Co 15:34; Eph 5:14. Also resurrection, from the sleep of death. Da 12:1-2.
AWL	Symbol of ear-mark of the love-slave. Ex 21:1-6.
AXE	Symbol of judgment, of warfare. "To cut." Lk 3:9; Jer 51:20; Eze 26:9; Mt 3:10.
BABYLON	Symbol of sin's confusion, apostasy. Ge 11; Rev 17,18; Rev 14:3. "Confusion."
BALANCE(S)	Symbol of honesty and just judgment. A pair of scales. Pr 11:1; 16:11; Job 31:6; Da 5:27.
BALDNESS	Symbol of weakness, humility. Isa 3:24; Lev 13:42-44; Jer 47:4-5; 48:27.
BALM	Symbol of healing ministry. Jer 8:22; 46:1.
BANNER	Symbol of standard lifted high. Isa 13:2.
BANQUETING	Symbol of festival time. SS 2:4.

BAPTISM Symbol of burial of old lifestyle. "To dip or immerse." Mt 3:11; Ro 6:1-11; Col 2:12,13; 1Co 12:13; Gal 3:27; Eph 4:5.

BARLEY Symbol of poverty, lowliness, low reputation. Passover harvest. Jdg 7:12; Nu 5:15; Hos 3:2; Eze 13:19; Ru 1:22.

BARN Symbol of storehouse, the kingdom to come. Mt 13:30; Job 39:12; Hag 2:19; Lk 12:24.

BARRENNESS Symbol of unproductivity. Isa 2:5; Ps 107:34.

BASKET Symbol of life's provisions. Mt 16:9,10; 15:37

BATHING Symbol of cleansing, purification. Lev 15:15; Eph 5:26; Tit 3:5; Jn 3:3-5.

BEAM Symbol of strength, support-rafter. Mt 7:3.

BEAR Symbol of evil, cunning and cruel men. "To move slowly." 1Sa 17:36; 2Sa 17:8; 2Ki 2:24; La 3:10; Pr 17:12; Hos 13:8; Am 5:19; Da 7:5; Rev 13:2.

BEAST (Wild) Symbol of world kingdoms; carnivorous, cruel, devouring. Da 7,8; Rev 13,17. Unclean animals.

BEAST (Domestic) Symbolic of Christ's sacrifice and the submissiveness of saints and clean animals. Lev chapters 1-7; Eph 5:1-2; Ro 12:1-2.

BEARD Symbol of strength, honor, age. Jer 48:36-38; Isa 7:20; Eze 5:1-6.

BED (Adultery) Symbol of spiritual fornication, idolatry, lusts. Jas 4:4; Rev 2:22.

BEES

Symbol of great hosts of people, stinging, yet produce honey. "Orderly." Dt 1:44; Jdg 14:8; Ps 118:12; Eze 3; Rev 10.

BELL

Symbol of a sweet sound. "Tinkling." Ex 28:24; Zec 14:20.

BELLY

Symbol of emotions, love and hate, etc. Pr 18:8; 20:27,30; Ps 31:9; SS 5:14; 7:2.

BIND

Symbol of conquering, subdue another. "To yoke or hitch." Mt 12:29; Jdg 15:10; 14:5; Job 39:10; Ps 105:22; Da 3:20; Mt 16:19; 18:18; Mk 5:3; Ac 22:4.

BIRD

Symbol of spirits, good or evil. "Covered with feathers." Clean birds - symbol of the Holy Spirit or saints. Mt 3:15-16. Unclean birds - symbol of evil spirits. Rev 18:2; Jer 4:25; Mt 13:32.

BLACK

Symbol of famine and death. La 5:10; Jer 14:1-2; Rev 6:5; La 4:4-8.

BLEMISH

Symbol of imperfections of human nature. Lev 21:18; 2Pe 2:13; Eph 5:25-28.

BLINDNESS

Symbol of spiritual ignorance, lack of discernment, insight. Ro 11:25; Isa 6:10; 42:18-19; Mt 15:14.

BLOOD

Symbol of the life of all flesh. Lev 17:11; Ge 9:5; 49:11; Heb 2:12; Isa 34:3; Mt 27:25.

BLUE

Symbol of heaven and authority. Ex 24:10; Eze 1:26; 10:1.

BODY

Symbol of structure, framework. Ro 12:5; 1Co 10:17; 12:12-27; Eph 2:16.

BOOK — Symbol of Divine revelation, or human thought. Writing, reading, eating of the book. Eze 3; Rev 10. God's Book - The Bible.

BOSOM — Symbol of love, affection, emotions. Jn 13:23; 1:18; Isa 40:11; Ps 89:50; Ru 4:16; Nu 11:12.

BOTTLE — Symbol of sustenance, source of supply. Ge 21:14-19; Jdg 4:19; 2Sa 16:1; Ps 56:8; Jos 9:4,13; Mt 9:17; Mk 2:22; Lk 5:37-38.

BOW — Symbol of judgment (with arrow). Ps 7:12; Job 6:4; Dt 32:23; Hab 3:11; 2Ki 13:14-19; Ps 38:2; 18:14; 64:3.

BRACELET — Symbol of betrothal, a pledge. Ge 24:22,30,37; 38:18; Isa 3:19; Eze 16:11.

BRAMBLE — Symbol of the curse, fruitlessness. Jdg 9:14,15; Lk 6:44; Isa 34:13.

BRANCHES (Palm) — Symbol of victory, rejoicing. Lev 23:40; Ne 8:15; Jn 12:13; SS 7:8; Jn 12:13. Feast of Tabernacles.

BRASS — Symbol of judgment against sin of disobedience, strength, endurance. Job 40:18; Da 7:19; Nu 21:5-10; Dt 33:25; Rev 1:15; Lev 26:19; Dt 28:23.

BREAD — Symbol of the staff of life. "Crushing, kneading." Jn 6:35-58; Ps 104:15; Mt 6:11.

BREAST — Symbol of love, nourishment, affection. Ex 29:26,27; Job 24:9; Isa 60:16; Jn 13:25; 21:20.

BREASTPLATE — Symbol of defense. Isa 59:17; Ex 25:7; Eph 6:14; 1Th 5:8.

BREATH
(or breathing)

Symbol of active life. Ge 2:7; 6:17; 7:15, 22; Ps 150:6; Eze 37:5-10; Da 5:23; Ac 17:25; Jn 20:22.

BRICK
(and slime)

Symbol of imitation stone, slavery and works of man. Ge 11:3; Ex 20:25; Isa 65:3.

BRIDLE

Symbol of restraint, control. Ps 32:9; 2Ki 19:28; Jas 3:2; Isa 30:28; 37:29; Eze 29:4.

BRIERS

Symbol of punishment, false teachings. Prickles. Jdg 8:7-16; Isa 5:5-7; 7:23; Eze 2:6; Heb 6:8.

BRIMSTONE

Symbol of punishment, torment. Rev 20:10; Dt 29:23; Job 18:15; Ps 11:16; Isa 30:33; Lk 17:29; Rev 9:17.

BROTHER

Type of likeness, character, relationship. Pr 18:9; Job 30:29; 1Co 5:11; Mt 12:50; Rev 1:9.

BUILDING

Symbol of a body, physical or spiritual structures. Pr 18:9; Job 30:28; 1Co 5:11; Mt 12:50; Lk 17:29.

BULLOCK

Symbol of strength, labor, servanthood. An ox. Pr 14:4; Ps 144:14; 22:12.

BURNT OFFERING

Symbol of voluntary sacrifice, freewill offering. Ps 40:6-8; Heb 9:11-14; 10:5-7; Php 2:8; Ro 12:1-2.

BUSH
(burning)

Symbol of humiliation, chastening, affliction. Ex 3:2-4; Isa 7:19; Jdg 9:15; Dt 4:20; Job 30:1-7.

CAIN

Type of natural, unregenerate man, worship of self-will. "A Lance." Ge 4:1-8; Jude 11; Heb 11:4.

CAKE	Symbol of worship, Divine food. Lev 7:12-13; Nu 15:20; Hos 7:8; Jer 7:18; 44:19. Leavened cakes - offering permeated by sinfulness of man. Unleavened cakes - offering without sin. Points to Christ.
CALF	Symbol of praise, thanksgiving. Hos 14:2 with Heb 13:15; Hos 13:2; Ge 18:7; Ex 32:4.
CAMEL	Symbol of service, servanthood, burden-bearer. Ge 24:64; Zec 14:15; Mt 19:24; 23:24; Lk 18:25. Yet not fit for food. Lev 11:4; Dt 14:7.
CANAAN	Symbol of inheritance gained by warfare. Jos 1:23; Heb 3,4.
CANDLE	Symbol of light. Used of the spirit of man, the Spirit of God, and the Word of God. Pr 20:27; Rev 4:5; Ps 119:105. A lamp-light.
CANDLESTICK	Symbol of light-bearers, Christ and the Church. Ex 25:31-35; Nu 3:31; Heb 9:2,11; Ps 119:130; Jn 1:1-9; 8:12; Mt 5:15; Rev 1:12-20.
CANKERWORM	Symbol of destructive powers. Joel 1:1; 2:25; Na 3:15,16.
CAPTAIN	Type of headship, leadership, Christ the Captain of our salvation. Heb 2:10; Jos 5:14; Da 8:11; Nu 31:14, 48.
CASSIA	Symbol of fragrance through crushing, suffering. Ps 45:8; Ex 30:24; Eze 27:19.
CATERPILLAR	Symbol of destructive powers. 1Ki 8:37; Ps 78:46; Isa 33:4; Joel 1:4; 2:25; 2Ch 6:28; Ps 105:34; Jer 51:14,27.

CEDAR	Symbol of power, majesty, beauty, royalty. Eze 17:1-23; 31:2-18; Isa 2:13; Ps 92:12; 80:10; 104:16; 148:9; SS 5:15.
CENSER (gold)	Symbol of prayer, intercession, praises. Lev 10:1; 16:12; Nu 16:17; Heb 9:4; Rev 8:1-5 with Ps 141:1-2.
CHAFF	Symbol of threshing away that which is now useless. Mt 3:12; Ps 1:4; Isa 5:24; 33:11; Jer 23:28. The wicked separated from righteous.
CHAIN	Symbol of binding, oppression, punishment. Fetters. Lam 3:7; Ps 149:8; Eze 7:23; Ps 73:6; Ac 28:20; 2Ti 1:16; Rev 20:1; Mk 5:3; 2Pe 2:4; Jude 6.
CHARIOT	Symbol of power, speed, transport in warfare. A vehicle. Ps 20:7; 104:3; Zec 6:1-2; Isa 66:15; Hab 3:8; Rev 9:9.
CHRIST	Type of Messiah, the Anointed One. All judges, kings, priests and O.T. "anointed ones" point to Him. Mk 1:1; Jn 1:41; Da 9:24-27.
CHEEK	Symbol of testing, suffering when smitten. Jos 6:10; 1Ki 22:24; Mt 5:39; Ps 3:7; Mic 5:1.
CHEW	Symbol of mediation on God's Word. Rev 10:9; Lev 11:3; Rev 2:7,14,17; Pr 9:17; Eze 18:2; 1Co 11:29; Pr 13:25.
CHILDREN	Type of immaturity, under guardianship, protection of infants. 1Co 13:11; 14:20; Eph 4:14; Heb 5:13; 1Pe 1:14; Mt 13:38; Lk 16:8.
CINNAMON	Symbol of fragrance. Pr 7:17; Ex 30:23; Rev 18:13.

CIRCLE

Symbol of endlessness, timeless, eternity. Isa 40:22; Ps 19:6. Circuit of the sun.

CIRCUMCISION

Symbol of covenantal relationship, cutting off the flesh life. Ge 17; Php 3:3; Ro 2:28-29; 4:11; Dt 10:16; 30:6; Lev 26:41; Col 2:11; Jer 4:4.

CISTERN

Symbol of man's water supply. 2Ki 18:31; Pr 5:15; Ecc 12:6; Isa 36:16; Jer 2:13.

CITY

Symbol of security, safety, permanency. Ge 4:17; 10:12; Jos 21:13; Heb 10:11-16; 12:22; 13:14; Rev 21,22.

CITIES
(of refuge)

Symbol of security and safety for a man-slayer. Jos 21 with Heb 6:18.

CLAPPING

Symbol of joy and rejoicing, exultation. Job 27:23; Ps 47:1; 98:8; Isa 55:12; La 2:15; Na 3:19; 2Ki 11:12; Eze 25:6.

CLAY

Symbol of frailty of human flesh, weakness of mankind. Isa 64:8; Job 13:12; 10:9; Da 2:33-45.

CLOKE
(or cloak)

Symbol of covering, whether clean or unclean. Jn 15:22; 1Th 2:5; 1Pe 2:16; Zec 3:4; Mt 5:40.

CLOSET

Symbol of secrecy, privacy, aloneness. Joel 2:16; Mt 6:6.

CLOUD and
FIERY PILLAR

Symbol of Divine covering, guidance, oversight, provision. Ex 13:21,22; Ps 18:11; 104:3; Isa 19:1; Eze 1:4; Mt 24:30; Rev 1:7; 1Th 4:17.

CLOVEN

Symbol of separation from the world in earth walk. Dt 14:7; Ac 2:3; Lev 11:3,7,26.

CLUSTER	Symbol of a group, a company, new wine. Isa 65:8; Mic 7:1; Nu 13:23,24; SS 1:14; Ge 40:10; Dt 32:32; Rev 14:18.
COAL	Symbol of burning fire, good or evil. SS 8:6; Pr 25:22; Ro 12:20; La 4:8; Isa 47:14; 6:6.
COCKATRICE	Symbol of Satan's evils or hosts. A viper. Isa 59:5; 14:29; 11:8; Jer 8:17.
COCK (rooster)	Symbol of warning, reminder. Mt 26:34,74, 75; Lk 22:34,60; Jn 13:38; 18:27.
COLT (donkey)	Symbol of burden-bearer, stubbornness, patience, endurance. Ge 49:11; Job 11:12; Zec 9:9; Mt 21:1-7; Jn 12:15.
COMMANDMENTS	Symbol of the Law of God. Ex 19:7; Dt 5:16,17; 26:13; Ps 103:18; Pr 4:4; Jn 15:10; 1Jn 3:22-24.
CONIES	Symbol of wisdom in hiding. Ps 104:18; Pr 30:24-26.
COPPER	Refer Brass.
CORD (scarlet)	Symbol of binding power. "To twist." Pr 5:22; Job 36:8; Ps 2:3; 118:27; 129:4; Eze 27:24.
CORN (Wine and Oil)	Symbol of harvest increase and blessing. Isa 28:28; 36:17; Ps 78:24; Jn 12:24. Ps 65:9,13; Hos 2:8,9,22; 1Ti 5:18.
CORNERSTONE	Symbol of foundation, alignment. Eph 2:20; Mt 21:42; 1Pe 2:6
CORNET	Symbol of calling, gathering together. 1Ch 15:28; Ps 98:6; Da 3:5-15; Hos 5:8; 2Sa 6:5.

COURT
(Outer)

Symbol of exclusion from inner place, tribulation period. Rev 11:1-3; Ex 27:9,12-19; 2Ch 4:9; Est 4:11; 5:1,2; Ps 65:4; 100:4; 135:2; Zec 3:7.

CRANE

Symbol of mourning, loneliness. Isa 38:14; Jer 8:7. A twitterer.

CRIMSON

Symbol of sin, suffering or sacrifice. Red, scarlet. Isa 1:18; Jer 4:30; 2Ch 2:7,14; 3:14.

CROOKED

Symbol of twistedness, not straight. Dt 32:5; Job 26:13; Ps 125:5; Pr 2:15; Ecc 1:15; Isa 40:4; 42:16; 59:8; La 3:9; Lk 3:5; Php 2:15.

CROSS
(stake)

Symbol of death, Christ crucified. Mt 16:24; 10:38; 1Co 1:17; Col 1:20; Gal 5:11; 6:12,14; Php 3:18; Heb 12:2.

CROWN

Symbol of eternal life, rewards, kingship, rulership. Rev 6:2; 13:7; 19:20; 2:10; 1Co 9:25; Jas 1:12; Pr 12:4. Crown of gold, crown of life.

CUD
(Chewing)

Symbol of meditation in God's Word. Lev 11:3-7; Dt 14:6-8.

CUMMIN

Symbol of smallness, seed life. Isa 28:25-27; Mt 23:23.

CUP

Symbol of life, health, or death and evil. Cup of the Lord, cup of devils, cup of abominations. Jn 18:11; Ps 11:6; 16:5; 23:5; Rev 17:4; Eze 23:33; Rev 14:10; Mt 26:38-42.

CYMBAL

Symbol of vibration, praise, worship. Ezr 3:10; Ne 12:27; Ps 150;5; 1Co 13:1; 2Sa 6:5; 1Ch 13:8, 15:16,19; 2Ch 29:25.

DANCE — Symbol of joy, rejoicing, whirling. Ps 30:11; Job 21:11; Ps 149:3; Ecc 3:4; Jer 31:13; La 5:15.

DARKNESS — Symbol of ignorance, blindness, sorrow, distress. Ex 10:21-23; Jn 8:12; Jn 1:5; 1Jn 2:8; Eph 5:8-11; Job 18:18; Col 1:13; 1Jn 2:11.

DAVID — Type of Christ, the anointed king, born in Bethlehem. 1 Sa 16:1,17; Mt 2:4,5. "Beloved".

DAY — Symbol of space, or a period of time. Isa 22:5; Ge 2:4; Joel 2:2; Jn 9:4; 2Pe 3:8; Ps 90:4.

DEAF — Symbol of inattentiveness, physically or spiritually. Isa 29:18; Ps 58:4; Isa 35:5; Mk 7:32-37; 9:25.

DESERT — Symbol of desolation, temptation, solitude. Jer 17:6; Isa 27:10; 33:9; 40:3; 21:1; Jer 50:12,39. Refer also to Wilderness.

DIAMOND — Symbol of hardness, brilliancy. Jer 17:1; Ex 28:18; 39:11; Eze 28:13; 3:9; Zec 7:12.

DISEASE — Symbol of calamity, sinfulness. Ps 103:3; Ecc 6:2; Ex 15:26; Dt 7:15; 28:60.

DOG — Symbol of unbelievers, religious hypocrites, yelpers. Php 3:2; Ps 22:16,20; Pr 26:11; 2Pe 2:22; Isa 56:10; Jer 15:3; Mt 7:6.

DOOR — Symbol of opening, entrance. 1Co 16:9; Hos 2:15; 2Co 2:12; Col 4:3; Jn 10:9; Rev 4:1; 3:8,20.

DOVE — Symbol of gentleness, the Holy Spirit. Pigeon. Mt 3:16; Jn 1:32; Mk 1:10; Lk 3:22.

DAWN

Symbol of a new day, fresh light after darkness. Mt 28:1; 2Pe 1:19; Jos 6:15; Job 7:4.

DRAGON

Symbol of Satan, the monster. Rev 12:7-9; 16:1; 13:2-4; 20:2; Ps 91;13; Isa 27:1; Jer 51:34.

DRINK

Symbol of imbibing, fellowship, whether good or evil. 1Co 10:4,21; 12:13; Ro 12:20; Jn 4:13-14; 7:37-39; Rev 14:8-10; 16:6, Mk 16:18.

DROSS

Symbol of refuse, dregs of impurity, wickedness, sin. Eze 22:18-19; Ps 119:119; Pr 26:23; Isa 1:25; Ps 75:8; Isa 51:17,22.

DRUNK

Symbol of being tipsy, overcome, under the power of sorrow, affliction, idolatry, delusions. Jer 51:7; Isa 63:6; Eze 23:33; Rev 17:2; Dt 32:42; Isa 49:26.

DUST

Symbol of humiliation, contempt, man's frailty. Isa 47:1; 1Sa 2:8; Na 3:18; Mt 10:4; Ac 13:51; Ps 71:9; 2Sa 16:3; Ac 22:33.

EAGLE

Symbol of swiftness of flight. Job 9:26; Dt 28:49; Pr 23:5; 30:10; Hab 1:8; Jer 48:40; Rev 12:14; Hos 8:11.

EAR

Symbol of hearing, either good or evil. Pr 28:9; 2:2; 4:20; Isa 1:10; 1Co 2:9; Job 13:1; Pr 17:4.

EARTHQUAKE

Symbol of judgment, shakings of God. Vibration. Rev 16:18-19; Isa 24:20; 29:6; Jer 4:24; Hag 2:6; Rev 6:12-13; 8:5.

EAST

Symbol of sunrise, God's light and glory arising. Ps 103:12; Rev 7:21; Ge 3:24; Rev 16:12; Eze 43:1,2.

EAT	Symbol of meditation, digestion of food. Jer 15:16; Eze 3:1-3; Rev 10:9; Lk 13:26; Dt 20:14; Mt 11:18.
EDEN	Symbol of pleasure, paradise, kingdom life. Eze 36:35; Ge 2:8-15; Joel 2:3.
EDIFY	Symbol of building, edifice. Eph 4:1-16; 1Co 14:4; 8:1.
EGYPT	Symbol of worldliness, bondage, whoredoms. Rev 11:8; Eze 23:3,4,8,19.
EIGHT	Symbol of new beginning, resurrection day. Jn 20:26; Lk 9:28-35; Ac 9:33; 1Pe 3:20; Ge 7:12; 2Pe 2:5.
EIGHTEEN	Symbol of judgment (double nine). Lk 13:11-16.
ELDERS (twenty-four)	Type of priesthood order. Priestly ministry. 1Ch 24; Rev 4:4,10.
ELEVEN	Symbol of incompleteness, disorder. One beyond ten, one short of twelve. Mt 20:6,9; 28:16; Mk 16:14; Ac 1:26; 2:14.
ELIJAH	Type of the prophetic Word of God. "My God is Jehovah." 1Ki 17,18; Mt 17:4; Lk 4:24-27.
ELISHA	Type of Christ as the Prophet with the double portion of the Spirit. 2Ki 5:10 with Mt 8:2; 2Ki 4:35 with Lk 8:50-56; 2Ki 7:16 with Mt 14:15-21.
EMERALD	Symbol of glories of God and His saints. Rev 4:3; 21:19.

ENSIGN — Symbol of protection, standard lifted high. A banner. Isa 11:12; 5:26; 18:3; 30:17; 31:9; Zec 9:16; Ps 74:4.

EPHOD — Symbol of priesthood ministry. Ex 28:2-8; Zec 6:13; Lev 16; Lk 12;37; Heb 4:14; 9:24.

ESAU — Type of sensual, profane, fleshly man. "Hairy". Heb 12:16; Ge 25:22-25; Ro 9:13.

EYE — Symbol of omniscience, knowledge, sight, insight, foresight. The seven eyes - perfection of sight. Ps 66:7; 12:15; Pr 16:2,30; 20:8; 19:8; 25:15; Rev 4:6; Ps 101:6.

EYESALVE — Symbol of anointing for healing the eyes. Rev 3:18 with 1Jn 2:20,27 and Jn 9:1-7

FACE — Symbol of character, countenance, image. Ge 1:26-29; Pr 21:29; Ge 3:19; Rev 4:7; 10:1; 22:4.

FAMINE — Symbol of judgment. Rev 18:18; Jer 5:12; Am 8:11,12; Jer 14:12-18; Eze 5:16-17.

FAN — Symbol of separation. Lk 3:17; Isa 41:16; Jer 15:7; Mt 3:12.

FAT — Symbol of energy, inward parts, warmth. Ps 92:14; 17:10; 119:70; Dt 32:15.

FEATHERS — Symbol of covering, protection. Ps 91:4; Eze 17:3,7; Da 4:33; Mt 23:37.

FEET — Symbol of walk, conduct. Feet on earth and sea. Formal possession. Gal 2:14; Ps 35:15; 1Sa 2:9; Ps 40:2; Rev 1:15.

FENCE — Symbol of protection, enclosure, restraint, safety. Isa 5:2; Ps 62:3; Nu 32:17.

FIELD

Symbol of the world, earth. Mt 13:24,38,44; Lk 15:15; Jn 4:35.

FIFTEEN

Symbol of the grace of the Godhead (3x5=15). 2Ki 20:6; Isa 38:5; Gal 1:18; Lk 3:1-6.

FIFTY

Symbol of liberty, freedom, Pentecost (10x5=50). 1Ki 18:4; Hag 2:14-16; Ac 2:1-4; Lev 23,25. The fiftieth day, fiftieth year.

FIG

Symbolic of fruit of Israel nation. Hab 3:17; Na 3:12; Isa 36:16; Jer 24:1-8; 29:17-18; Lk 13:6-9.

FIG-LEAVES

Symbolic of self-atonement, self-made covering. Ge 3:1-8; Isa 64:6.

FIG TREE

Symbolic of national and political life of Israel. Mt 24:32-33; Jdg 9:10; SS 2:13,14; Lk 21:29-33; Rev 6:13; Mt 21:19-21; Mk 11:13-21; Lk 13:6,7.

FINGER OF GOD

Symbol of work of God, the Holy Spirit in conviction. Ex 8:19; 29:12; 31:18; Dt 9:10; Lk 11:20,46.

FIRE

Symbol of presence, burning judgment of God, purifying, testing. Heb 12:29; Ge 19:24; Ex 3:2; 2Ki 1:10-14; Da 7:9; Isa 66:15; 2Th 1:7-8. Holiness of God.

FIVE

Symbol of God's grace to man, responsibility of man. 1SA 17:40; Mt 14:17-21; 25:2,15-20; Lk 19:18,19.

FISH

Symbol of souls of men. Mt 4:19; Eze 29:4,5; Mt 13:48; Heb 1:14.

FLAX

Symbol of weakness of man. Mt 12:20.

FLIES	Symbol of evil spirits, filth of Satan's kingdom. Beelzebub - "Lord of flies." Ex 8; Mt 10:25.
FLOCK	Symbol of the people of God. Isa 40:11; Jn 10:16; Ps 100:1-5.
FLOOD	Symbol of judgment on sin and violence. The Deluge. Isa 59:19; Ge 6:17; Ps 29:10.
FLOOR	Symbol of earth. Lk 3:17; Hos 9:2; Mic 4:12; Mt 3:12; Joel 2:22-27.
FLOUR	Symbol of broken body of Jesus. "To grind." Isa 53; 28:28; Lev 2:1; Nu 28:5; 1Ch 23:29.
FLOWER	Symbol of fading glory of man. Jas 1:10,11; 1Pe 1:24; Isa 40:1-3.
FOOL	Type of Antichrist and followers. Wicked, vile, perverse people. Ps 14:1; 1Sa 26:21; Pr 17:7-28; Lk 12:20.
FOOT	Refer to Feet.
FOREHEAD	Symbol of thought, reason, mind, memory, imagination. Rev 14:9; Ex 28:38; 1Sa 17:49; 2Ch 26:19; Eze 9:4; Rev 7:3; 13:16; 22:4.
FOREIGNER	Type of stranger, one without citizenship. Eph 2:12,19; 1Pe 2:11; Php 3:20; Ps 119:19; Pr 2:16; 5:10; 6:1; Jn 10:5; Heb 11:13.
FOREST	Symbol of nations. A thicket. Eze 15:1-6; 20:46-49; Hos 2:12; isa 44:23; Jer 12:8; 21:4.
FORNICATION	Symbol of spiritual idolatry. Rev 14:9; 17:2-4; 18:3; 19:2; 2:21; 1Co 6:9.

FORTRESS (or Tower)   Symbol of protection, a stronghold. Ps 31:3; 18:2; 71:3; 91:2; 2Sa 22:2; Isa 17:3; Jer 6:27; 16:19; Isa 34:13; 25:12; 33:16.

FORTY   Symbol of testing, trial, closing in victory or defeat (10x4=40). Ge 7:4,17; Ex 16:35; Ps 95:10; Mt 4:2; Lk 4:2; Ac 7:23,36; 2Co 11:24; Heb 3:9,17.

FOWL   Symbol of spirits, good or evil. Rev 18:2; Mk 4:32.

FOUNDATION   Symbol of beginning. Eph 2:20; Job 4:17-21; Mt 13:35; 25:34; Isa 28:16; 1Co 3:11; Heb 6:1-2; Jer 17:13; Rev 21:6.

FOUNTAIN   Symbol of life source, a gushing forth. Ps 36:9; Ge 8:28; Pr 13:14; 14:27; Ecc 12:5-7; Jer 2:13; 17:13; Rev 21:6; Jn 4:14.

FOUR   Symbol of worldwide, universal. Isa 11:12; Ge 2:10; Da 7:6,17; Jer 49:36; Mt 15:38; 16:10; Mk 2:3; 13:27; Jn 11:17,39; Rev 7:1; 20:8.

FOURTEEN   Symbol of Passover, of testing (10+4=14). Ex 12:6; Nu 9:5; Ge 31:41; Ac 27:27-33; Mt 1:17.

FOX   Symbol of cunning, evil men. A Burrower. Lk 13:32; Eze 13:1,2; SS 2:15.

FRANKINCENSE   Symbol of fragrance, prayers, intercession. "White". Lev 2:1,2; Nu 5:5; SS 3:6; Ex 30:34; Rev 18:13; Mt 2:11.

FROG   Symbol of demons, unclean spirits. Ex 8; Rev 16:13; Ps 78:45.

FRUIT   Symbol of increase or multiplication. Ps 21:10; Ex 21:22; Hos 9:16; Dt 7:13; Ac 2:30; Ps 132:11; Jer 17:10; Pr 12:14; 18:20; Heb 13:15; Gal 5:22,23; Eph 5:9; Php 1:11.

FURNACE   Symbol of trial, testing. A fire-pot. Pr 17:3; Dt 4:20; 1Ki 8:51; Ps 12:6; Isa 31:9; 48:10; Jer 11:4.

GALL   Symbol of bitterness. A poisonous plant. Ac 8:23; Dt 32:32; Am 6:12; Ps 69:21; Jer 8:14; 9:5; 23:15; La 3:5,19.

GARDEN   Symbol of growth and fertility. Isa 58:11; Ge 2:8-10.

GARMENT   Symbol of covering, evil or righteous, defiled or beautiful. Ps 73:6; 104:2; 109:19; Isa 64:6; Jer 43:12; Mal 2:16; Zec 13:4; Da 7:9; Mk 10:50; 16:5; Jude 23; Rev 1:13.

GATE   Symbol of entrance, power, authority. Ge 19:1; 22:17; 24:60; Ex 32:26,27; Heb 13:12; Ps 24:7; 100:4; 107:16; 122:2; Mt 16:18.

GIDEON   Type of Christ the Deliverer. "Cutter down, Warrior." Jdg 7,8.

GIRDLE   Symbol of strength for action. A belt. Lk 12:35; Job 30:11; Isa 45:5; 22:21; 1Pe 1:13; Ps 18:39; Job 12:18; Ps 65:6.

GLORY   Symbol of Presence of God. The Shekinah Glory. Ex 40:34,35; Eze 43:1-3.

GOAT   Symbol of sin, sinners, sin-offering. "Shaggy." Mt 25:32:33; 2Co 5:21; Lev 4:12; Isa 16:15,27; Nu 28:22; Eze 43:25.

GOG/MAGOG   Symbolic of godless masses of wicked. Eze 38,39; Rev 20:1-8.

145

GOLD	Symbol of kingship, kingdom glory, God or gods. Rev 14:14; SS 5:11; Da 3:1; Mt 2:11; Ac 17:29; 1Co 3:12; Rev 4:4; 9:7; 18:9-12; Mal 3:3; Hag 2:8.
GOURD	Symbol of earth's temporary product. Jnh 4:6-10.
GOMORRAH	Symbol of wickedness, idolatry, immorality, pride, prosperity. Eze 16:49; 2Pe 2:6; Ge 13:10; Rev 14:10,11; Mk 6:1; Jude 7.
GRAPES	Symbol of fruit of the vine. Isa 5:2; Jn 15:1; Ge 40:10,11; 49:11; Nu 13:20-24; SS 2:15; 7:7; Rev 14:18.
GRASS	Symbol of frailty of the flesh. Ps 9:5; Isa 40:6-8; 51:12; Job 5:25; Ps 37:2; 72:16; 92:7; 102:4,11; 103:15; 1Pe 1:24.
GRASSHOPPER	Symbol of multitudes, smallness of size. A locust. Jdg 6:5; Nu 13:33; Isa 40:22; Jer 46:23; Am 7:1; Na 3:17; Jdg 7:12.
GREY	Symbol of dignity, honor, age. Pr 16:31; Ge 42:38; 44:29-31; Dt 32:25; Hos 7:9; 1Sa 12:2; Job 15:10; 41:32; Ps 78:18; 71:18; Pr 20:29.
GREEN	Symbol of prosperity, growth, life. Ps 23:2; Ge 1:30; Ex 10:15; Job 8:16; SS 2:13; Jer 17:2; Mk 6:39; Lk 23:31.
GRIND	Symbol of oppression, servitude. "To chew up." Isa 3:15; 47:2; Job 31:10; Jdg 16:21; La 5:13.
HAIL	Symbol of Divine judgment. Ps 78:47; Ex 9:18-34; Ps 18:13; 105:32; Isa 28:2; 32:19; Rev 8:7; 11:19; 16:21.

146

HAIR — Symbol of glory of man or beast. Jdg 16:17,22; Isa 3:24; Jer 7:29; 1Co 11:14,15; Jn 11:2; Lk 7:38.

HAMMER — Symbol of Word of God. "To pound." Jer 23:29.

HAND — Symbol of strength, power, action, possession. Hand lifted up. Left hand. Right hand. Jn 10:28; Ps 90:17; Job 9:30; 1Ti 2:8; Isa 1:15; Ex 15:26; Ps 17:7; 16:8; 109:31; 110:5; Mk 14:62.

HARE — Symbol of Satan, evil hosts, uncleanness. Lev 11:6; Dt 14:7.

HARLOT — Typical of idolater, adulteress. Rev 17:1; Isa 1:21; Jer 2:20; Rev 17:5,15; 19:2.

HARP — Symbol of praise, worship to God. "To twang." Ps 150:3; 33:2; 43:4; 71:22; 147:7; Rev 14:2,3; 15:2.

HART (Deer) — Symbol of gentleness, timidity, sensitivity. SS 2:9,17.

HARVEST — Symbol of gathering, reaping, righteous or wicked. Mt 13:30; Rev 14:14-20; Lev 23.

HAWK — Symbol of uncleanness, scavenger. Lev 11:16; Dt 14:15; Job 39:26.

HAY — Symbol of little worth. Isa 15:16; 1Co 3:12.

HEAD — Symbol of thoughts, mind, intelligence, rulership, lordship. Isa 15; Mt 22:37; Ex 29:10; Lev 1:4; 3:2; 1Co 11:3; Eph 1:22; 5:23-24.

HEART   Symbol of center of being, life, emotions, motivations. 1Ti 1:5; Ps 40:8-12; 1Co 7:37; Ro 6:17; Pr 25:20; Lev 19:7.

HEAT   Symbol of burden, trial, persecution. Mt 20:12; Rev 16:9; Mt 13:6; Lk 8:6-13; Job 30:30; Eze 3:4; Da 3:19; Jas 1:11.

HEDGE   Symbol of protection, restrain, restriction. A wall. Job 1:10; Isa 5:5; Eze 13:5; Mk 12:1; Job 3:23; Ps 80:12; Mt 21:33.

HEEL   Symbol of power to crush. Ge 3:15; Ro 16:20.

HEIFER (red)   Symbol of consecration, purification by sacrifice. Nu 19.

HELMET   Symbol of protection for the head. Eph 6:17; Isa 59:17; 1Th 5:8.

HEN   Symbolic of motherhood, one who gathers, protects. Mt 23:37; Lk 13:34.

HERB (bitter)   Symbol of sufferings and bitterness. Nu 9:11; Job 10:1; Pr 14:10; Ex 12:8; Heb 6:7.

HIDING   Symbol of sin, or secrecy. Ps 9:15; Ge 3:8-10; Ps 32:5; 35:7,8, 119:11; Isa 28:15; 49:2; 59:2; Mt 13:33,34; 25:18; Jn 8:39; Rev 6:15.

HILLS   Symbol of elevation, high, loftiness. Ps 68:16; Ge 7:19; Ps 95:4; 98:8.

HIND   Symbol of swiftness, agility. Fallow deer. 2Sa 22:34; Ps 18:33; Hab 3:19; SS 2:17; Isa 35:6.

HONEY   Symbol of natural sweetness; good, but not for God's altar. Ps 19:10; 81:16; 119:103; Pr 25:27; 24:13; Eze 3:13; Rev 10:9.

HORN

Symbol of power, strength, defense. Ps 18:2; Hab 3:4; Lk 1:69; Rev 17:12; 5:6; 13:1; Ps 22:21; 75:10; 132:17; Eze 29:21; 1Sa 2:10; Ps 89:17; La 2:3.

HORSE

Symbol of power, strength, conquest. Jer 8:6; 4:29; Ps 66:12; Job 39:19; Pr 21:31; Zec 10:3; Rev 19:19; Eze 38:4.

HOUSE

Symbol of home, dwelling place, the church. Jn 14:2; Job 30:23; Isa 14:18; 2:2-4; 2Co 5:1; Heb 3:1-6.

HUSBAND

Type of headship, protection, bonder of household. Eph 5:23; Jn 15:1; 1Co 3:9; Isa 54:5; 1Pe 3:1.

HYSSOP

Symbol of purification, applied by faith. Ps 51:7; Lev 14:4,49-52; Nu 19:6,18; Heb 9:19.

INCENSE

Symbol of prayer, intercessions. Refer Frankincense. Ps 141:2; Jer 1:16; 11:12,13; Lk 1:10,11; Rev 5:8; 8:3,4; Isa 60:6.

IRON

Symbol of strength, affliction, judgment, inflexible rule, crushing. Da 2:33; Ps 107:10; Jdg 4:3; Ps 2:5,9; Rev 2:27; Da 7:7,19; Dt 33:25; Mic 4:13; Job 40:18; Lev 26:19; Rev 12:5.

ISAAC

Type of Christ, only begotten son and sacrifice. "Laughter." Ge 22:2 with Jn 3:16; Gal 3:16; 4:22-31; Isa 9:6; Heb 1:1-4; Php 2:5-12; Heb 2:9.

ISRAEL

Type of true and spiritual Israel of God, having power with God and men. Ge 32; Gal 6:16; Ro 9:1-13.

ISLES

Symbol of Gentile nations of the earth. Ge 10:5; Zep 2:11; Isa 41:1; 42:12,15; Ac 28:1,7.

IVORY	Symbol of beauty and strength. Ps 45:8; 1Ki 10:18; SS 5:14; 7:4; Eze 27:15; Am 3:15; Rev 18:12.
JACOB	Type of Christ and believers, the spiritual replacing the natural. "Supplanter." The shepherding one. Ge 31:39,40; Isa 40:11; Jn 4:6-13; Jn 10.
JASPER	Symbol of glory of God, brightness, beauty. Rev 4:3; 21:11,18,19; Ex 28:20.
JAWS	Symbol of strength, power. Jawbone. Isa 30:28; Jdg 15:16; Job 29:17; Eze 29:4.
JERICHO	Symbol of city of palm trees. Dt 34:3.
JERUSALEM	Symbol of city of God, dwelling place of God and the saints. "The Foundation of Peace." Heb 12:22-28; Gal 4:6; Rev 3:12, 21:2,10.
JEWELS	Symbol of special treasures, the people of God. Mal 3:17; 1Co 3:12; Ex 19:5; Dt 14:2; Ps 135:4; 1Pe 2:9; Tit 2:14. Peculiar people.
JOB	Type of persecuted saints, trial, patience under suffering. Jas 5:11; Job 1,2,40.
JONAH	Type of death, burial, resurrection of Christ, ministry among the Gentiles. Mt 12:40; 16:4; Lk 11:30; Jnh 1:15-17; 2:1-10.
JORDAN	Symbol of descending, dying to self, going down. 2Ki 5:10; Mk 1:9.
JOSEPH	Type of Jesus as beloved, rejected, exalted Son with Gentile bride. "He shall add." Ge 37; Ac 7:9; Ps 105:16-22; Ac 2:36; Php 3:5-11; Lk 1:32,33; Zec 12:10.

JOSHUA
: Type of Jesus as Captain, leader into inheritance. Jos 1:5; Ac 7:45; Heb 4:8; Nu 25:18; Ex 33:7-11. Joshua = "Jesus/Savior".

JUDAS ISCARIOT
: Type of Antichrist, Son of Perdition, betrayer. Jn 17:12; 2Th 2:3-8; Rev 17:11.

KEY
: Symbol of authority, power to bind or loose, lock or unlock. Key of David, Death and Hades, Kingdom, Bottomless Pit, Knowledge. Isa 22:22; Rev 3:7; Mt 16:19; 18:18; Lk 11:52; Rev 9:1; 20:1.

KIDNEY
: Symbol of desire, emotions. Pr 23:16; Job 16:13; Ps 16:7; Job 19:27.

KINE
: Symbol of wealth. Refer Kine/Cow. Dt 7:13; Am 4:1; Ge 41:2,26-29; Dt 28:4; 2Sa 17:29.

KING
: Type of ruler, possessor of supreme power, Christ Jesus. 1Ti 1:17; Pr 8:15,16; Jn 1:49; 18:33-36; 1Ti 6:15,16; Rev 1:6; Da 7:22-27; Mt 19:28; 27:11; Rev 19:16.

KNEE
: Symbol of reverence, humility, bended knee. Ro 14:11; Ge 41:3; Isa 45:23; Mt 27:29; Ro 11:4; Php 2:19; Eph 3:14.

LADDER
: Symbol of Christ connecting heaven and earth. Ge 28:12; Jn 1:51.

LAMB
: Symbol of Christ our perfect sacrifice, Passover Lamb. Ex 12; 1Pe 1:19; Jn 1:29,36; Isa 53:6,7; Rev 5:6; Isa 40:11; Ac 8:32.

LAME
: Symbol of imperfection. Pr 26:7; 2Sa 5:8; Lev 21:17-23; Job 29:15; Isa 35:6.

LAMP	Symbol of spirit of man, Spirit of God, Word of God, salvation. Refer to Candle. Pr 20:27; Ps 119:105; Pr 6:23; Isa 62:1; Rev 1:14; Da 10:6 2Sa 22:29; Ps 18:28.
LAND	Symbol of earth, man's dwelling place. Ge 1:9,10; 2:11-13.
LAUGH	Symbol of gladness, joy or mockery. Ps 59:8; Pr 1:26; 2:4; 22:7; 37:13; 80:6; 126:2,3; Job 5:20; Ge 18:11-15; 2Ch 30:10.
LEAF	Symbol of life amidst prosperity or adversity. Ps 1:3; Isa 1:30; 34:4; 64:6; Jer 17:8; Mt 24:32; Rev 22:2.
LEAVEN	Symbol of evil doctrine, practices, life, teaching. Fermented. Action arrested by fire. Mt 8:15; Ex 12:15; Lev 2:11; Mt 16:6-12; Dt 16:3,4; 1Co 5:6-8.
LEBANON	Symbol of beauty, strength, loftiness. Isa 60:13; 10:34; 29:17; Jer 22:6,23; Hab 2:17; Isa 35:2; Ps 90:12; Isa 2:13.
LEEKS (garlic or onions)	Symbol of Egypt's food, world produce. Nu 11:5.
LEGS	Symbol of man's walk, man's strength, or animal strength. Dt 28:15, 35; Ex 29:17; Pr 26:7; Da 2:33; Jn 19:31; Ge 18:4; Ps 147:10.
LEOPARD	Symbol of swiftness, cruelty, vengeance, ferocity. "Spotted one." Jer 5:6; Da 7:6; Hab 1:8; Rev 13:2.
LEPROSY	Symbol of sin, transgression. Mt 8:3; 2Ch 26:19; Mk 1:42; Lk 5:12,13; Lev 13:44; Nu 12:10; 2Ki 5:27.

LETTER Symbol of the Law of Moses. Ro 2:27-29; 7:6; 2Co 3:6,7.

LIGHT Symbol of God, of Christ. 1Jn 1:5; Jas 1:17; Ps 104:2; 1Ti 6:14-16; Jn 1:14; Ps 18:11; Mt 4:16; Jn 8:12; 12:35, 36; 2Co 4:6; Eph 5:14; 1Pe 2:9; Ps 27:1; 119:105; Mt 5:14; Eph 5:8. Symbol of the Christian Church.

LIGHTNING Symbol of majesty of God, God coming into activity in earth. Associated with thunders, voices and earthquake. Da 10:6; Ex 19:16; Eze 1:14; Mt 24:27; 28:3; Lk 10:18; Rev 8:5; 11:19; 16:18.

LILIES Symbol of beauty, splendor. Mt 6:28, 29; SS 5:13; 7:2; Lk 12:27; 1Ki 7:19-22; SS 2:1,2; Hos 14:5.

LINEN (fine) Symbol of moral purity, righteousness. Ro 15:6; Ge 41:42; Rev 19:8,14.

LION Symbol of kingship, royalty, courage, boldness, of good and evil persons. Rev 5:5; 1Pe 5:8; Jdg 14:18; 1Sa 1:23; Ge 49:9; Nu 24:9; 2Sa 17:10; Pr 28:1; Hos 5:14; 13:8.

LIPS Symbol of testimony. Ps 63:5; Ex 6:12; Jos 2:10; Ps 12:2,3; 51:15; 34:13; 66:14; 71:23; 119:13; 140:3-9; Pr 10:21; 18:6; Heb 13:15.

LOAVES (two wave loaves) Symbol of Jews and Gentiles accepted of God in Christ. Lev 23:15-22; 1Co 12:13; Eph 2:11-22.

LOCUST Symbol of destructive enemy powers. Rev 9:3; Na 3:17; Isa 33:4; Rev 9:7.

LOINS Symbol of strength in action. Job 40:16; 38:3; Ps 66:11; Pr 31:17; Isa 11:5; Na 2:1; Mt 3:4; Lk 12:35; Eph 6:14; 1Pe 1:13.

153

LOT   Type of backslider. 2Pe 2:7,8; Ge 13:1-14;
                     19:1-36; Lk 17:28,29.

MAN   Type of the image and likeness of God. Ge
                     1:26-28; 1Co 15:45-50; Eze 1:10. King of
                     creation.

MANNA   Symbol of Christ the Bread of Life. "What
(gold pot)   is it?" Ex 16:14,15; Dt 8:3; Jn 6:30-57; Rev
                     2:17. Word by the Spirit.

MANTLE   Symbol of spiritual covering, good or evil. A
                     robe. Ps 109:29; 2Ki 2:13-15; 1Ki 19:19;
                     1Sa 28:13,14; 15:27.

MARBLE   Symbol of kingdom beauty. 1Ch 29:2; Est
                     1:6; SS 5:15; Rev 18:12.

MARK   Symbol to distinguish, sign, identification.
                     Mark of the Beast. Ge 4:15; Eze 9:4-6; Ro
                     16:17. Mark of God. Rev 13:16,17; 14:9-11;
                     15:2; 16:2; 19:20; 20:4; 14:1; 7:3; 22:4.

MARRIAGE   Symbol of union of two, two become one.
(of the Lamb)   Rev 19:7; Eph 5:23-32; Ge 1:26-28; 2:21-25;
                     Mt 19:4-6.

MEAT   Symbol of strong food, good or evil. Jn 4:34;
                     Ps 42:3; Jn 6:27; 1 Co 3:2; 10:3; Heb 5:12-
                     14; Job 6:7; 20:14.

MEAT OFFERING   Symbol of Christ Jesus offered to God as
                     man's food. Lev 2:1; Isa 28:28.

MELCHIZEDEK   King of Righteousness, King of Peace.
                     Christ Jesus. Pre-incarnate Christ. Heb
                     6:20; 5:6-10; 7:1-21; Ge 14:17-20; Ps 110.

MERCY SEAT   Symbol of atonement, appeasement, meeting
                   place of God and man, mediatorial.   Ex
                   25:22; 29:42,43; Nu 7:89; Ro 3:24,25; Heb
                   9:11,12; 1Jn 2:2; 2Co 5:20; 1Ti 2:5.

MESSENGER   Type of Christ, God's ultimate and perfect
                   messenger.   Mal 3:1,2; Jn 1:1-4,14-18.
                   God's Word.

MIDNIGHT   Symbol of end of the age, change of time,
                   new beginning.   Jdg 6:3; Job 34:20; Ps
                   119:62; Mt 25:6; Ac 16:25; 20:7; Ru 3:8; Ex
                   11; Ac 27:27.

MILK   Symbol of foundation food, first principle for
                   the young. 1Co 3:2; Heb 5:12,13; 1Pe 2:2.

MIRE   Symbol of man's works, and filth.   Ps
                   69:2,14.

MIRACLE   Symbol of supernatural power, good or evil.
                   Jn 3:2; 6:3; Ac 2:22; 15:12; Gal 3:5; Rev
                   16:14; 13:14; 19:20.

MOON   Symbol of light in darkness, sign of the Son
(to blood)   of Man. Church shines in the darkness. Php
                   2:15; Rev 12:1; Job 31:26; Ge 37:9; Ps
                   121:6.

MORNING   Symbol of new day, sunrise. Isa 58:8; Ps
                   30:5; 130:6; Jer 21:12; Da 8:26; Rev 2:27,28;
                   22:16.

MOSES   Type of Christ, Deliverer, Mediator, Prophet,
                   Sent One, Lawgiver. "Drawn out of water."
                   Dt 18:18; Heb 3:1-6; Ac 7:23-28; 1Ti 2:5; Nu
                   12:6-8.

MOTH   Symbol of destruction. Job 13:28; 27:18; Ps
                   39:11; Isa 50:9; 51:8; Hos 5:12; Mt 6:19,20;
                   Lk 12:33; Jas 5:2.

MOUNTAIN	Symbol of strength, majesty, stability, a kingdom of God or of man. Isa 2:2; Da 2:35; Jer 51:25; Zec 4:7; Ps 72:3.
MOUTH	Symbol of testimony, good or evil. Col 3:8; Ps 62:4; 63:5,11; 71:8; 51:5; Pr 2:6; 8:7; Mt 4:4; 12:34; Ac 3:18-21; 8:35; Ro 3:14,19; Eph 6:19; Rev 1:16; 19:15-21.
MULE	Symbol of stubbornness. Refer Ass/Donkey. Ps 32:9.
MUSIC	Symbol of joy, praise, worship. 1Sa 18:6; 2Ch 7:6; La 3:63; Da 3:5-7; Lk 15:25-32.
MUSTARD (seed)	Symbol of smallness to unnatural growth. Mt 13:31; Lk 13:19; Mt 17:20; Mk 4:31; Lk 17:6.
MYRRH	Symbol of suffering, fragrance. Ps 45:7,8; Pr 7:17; SS 1:13; 3:6; 4:6,14; 5:1-5; Mt 2:11; Jn 19:39.
MYRTLE TREE	Symbol of God's blessings. Isa 41:19; Ne 8:15; Zec 14:16.
NAIL	Symbol of sure fastening. A Peg. Ecc 12:11; Jdg 4:21,22; 1Ch 22:3; Isa 41:1-7; Jer 10:4; Jn 20:25; Col 2:14; Isa 22:20-25; Ezr 9:8.
NAKED	Symbol of being stripped, undone, exposed. Hab 3:9; 2Ch 28:19; Job 22:6; Rev 3:17; 17:16; Ac 19:16.
NAME (new)	Symbol of character, title, position, distinction. Mt 1:21, Jesus/Savior. Mk 14:61, Christ/Anointed One. Rev 2:17; 3:12. Refer Symbolic Names.

NAZARITE — Symbol of separation consecration. "Separated One.". Jdg 16:5-7,17; Nu 6:2-21; Am 2:11,12.

NECK — Symbol of strength, beauty, or stubbornness, humility or hardness of spirit. Pr 29:1; Ge 27:40; Ex 13:13; Dt 28:48; 31:27; SS 7:4; Isa 48:4; Jer 17:23; Hos 10:11.

NEST — Symbol of dwelling place, a home. Pr 27:8; Nu 24:21; Dt 22:6; 31:11; Job 29:18; 39:27; Ps 84:3; Isa 16:2; 34:15; Jer 22:23; 48:28; 49:16; Hab 2:9.

NET — Symbol of a catcher. Ps 10:9; Job 18:8; 19:6; Ps 9:15; 25:15; 31:4; 35:7,8; 57:6; 66:11; Pr 1:17; 29:5; Eze 12:13; Mic 7:2; Mt 13:47; Jn 21:6-11.

NIGHT — Symbol of spiritual darkness, tribulation period. Jn 11:10; 9:4; Lk 5:5; 17:34; Jn 3:2; Ro 13:12; 1Th 5:2-7; 2Pe 3:10; Rev 8:12; 21:25; 22:5.

NINE — Symbol of judgment, finality (last of digit figures). 2Ki 17:6; Lev 23:32; 2Ki 18:10; 25:1-3; Ezra 10:9; Jer 25:4-6; Eze 24:1-3; Mt 20:5; 27:45-46; Lk 23:44.

NORTH — Symbol of power, majesty, judgment; God's throne. "Gloomy." Job 37:9; 26:7; Ps 48:2; 89:12; 107:3; Pr 25:23; Isa 14:13; 41:25; Jer 1:13-15; 4:6; Da 11:6-44.

NOSE — Symbol of breath, discernment. The nostril. Job 4:9; Pr 30:30; 2Ki 19:28; Ex 15:8; 2Sa 22:9,16; Ps 18:8; Job 39:20.

OAK — Symbol of strength. Am 2:9; Isa 1:30; 2Sa 18:9-14.

157

OFFSPRING	Type of fruitfulness, blessing, reproduction. Ps 127, 128; Rev 22:16; Mt 1:1. Offspring of David - Jesus Christ.
OIL	Symbol of Holy Spirit in anointing. Lk 4:17; Isa 61:1; Ps 23:5; Ac 19:38; 1Jn 2:20,27; 2Co 1:21; Lev 2:1-2; Dt 33:24.
OINTMENT	Symbol of anointing (as above).
OLIVE TREE	Symbol of the anointing. The oily tree. Spiritual life in Israel and the church. Ps 52:8; 128:3; Jer 11:16; Hos 14:6; Ro 11:17-24; Isa 41:19.
ONE	Symbol of beginning, God, the source of all, unity of God's being, Divine sovereignty. Jn 8:41,50; 10:16; 18:13; Dt 6:4; Ps 71:22; Isa 60:9.
ONE-HUNDRED FORTY-FOUR	Symbol of God's ultimate in creation. Rev 7:1-3; 14:1-4.
ONE HUNDRED FIFTY-THREE	Symbol of revival, ingathering, final harvest of souls. Jn 21.
OVEN	Symbol of fiery trials, testing, or judgment. Fire-pot. Ps 21:9; Hos 7:4-7; Mal 4:1; Mt 6:30; Lk 12:28; Ex 8:3.
OVERSHADOW	Symbol of God's Presence and power. "To envelope in a shadow." Mt 17:5; Lk 1:35; Ac 5:15; Mk 9:7; Lk 9:34.
OWL	Symbol of evil spirits, demons, a night bird. Isa 13:21; Job 30:29; Isa 34:13; 43:20; Jer 50:30.
OXEN	Symbol of labor, servanthood. Am 6:12; Ps 144:14; Pr 14:4; Isa 1:3; 1Co 9:9; 1Ti 5:18.

PALACE | Symbol of heaven, God's dwelling place (not a tent). Ps 45:8; 78:69; Jn 14:1,2.

PALE | Symbol of death and disease. Rev 6:8; Jer 30:6; Isa 29:22.

PALM TREE | Symbol of victory. Refer Palm. Ps 92:12; SS 7:7,8; Jn 12:13.

PALMERWORM | Symbol of destructive powers. Joel 1:4; 2:25; Am 4:9.

PARADISE | Symbol of heaven. Third heaven. Most holy place. Rev 2:7; 2Co 12:2-4.

PASSOVER | Type and symbol of deliverance by the Lamb of God from bondage of Satan and sin. Ex 12:11; 1Co 5:7; Jn 1:29,36; Ro 3:25,26.

PASTURE | Symbol of feeding ground, Christ the Shepherd. Ps 79:13; 95:7; 100:3; Jer 23:1; Lam 1:6; Eze 34:14,31; Jn 10:1; Ps 23:2.

PAW | Symbol of unclean power. 1 Sa 17:37; Lev 11:26-28.

PEACE OFFERING | Symbol of Christ as Peace-Maker, Reconciler between God and Man. Col 1:20; Lev 3; Jn 14:27; 16:33; Ro 16:20; Eph 2:14-17.

PEARL | Symbol of God's truths, God's people, formed through suffering. Mt 7:6; 13:45,46; Rev 17:4; Rev 21:21.

PELICAN | Symbol of a lonely person. Ps 102:6,7.

PIGEON | Symbol of a mourner, sacrifice. Refer Dove. Isa 59:11; Lev 1:14; Ge 15:9; Lev 15:14,29.

PILLAR | Symbol of strength, firmness, support. Jer 1:18; 1Ti 3:15; Rev 3:12; SS 5:15; Gal 2:9; Rev 10:1.

PINE TREE — Symbol of fragrance, beauty. Ne 8:15; Isa 41:19; 60:13.

PIT — Symbol of prison, bondage. Isa 14:15; 24:22; 38:17,18; Jer 18:20; Rev 9:1,2; 20:1-3.

PITCHER — Symbol of a vessel, the human body. La 4:2; Ge 24:14-20; Ecc 12:6; Jdg 7:16-20; 2Co 3:2-11. Earthen vessel.

PLATTER — Symbol of hypocrisy, externalism. Lk 11:39; Mt 23:25,26.

PLUMBLINE — Symbol of measuring, Divine standard. Am 7:7,8.

PLOW — Symbol of breaking open, preparation for sowing. Jer 4:3; Job 4:8; Pr 20:4; 1Co 9:10; Hos 10:13; Ps 129:3; Am 9:13; Pr 21:4.

POISON — Symbol of evil teachings. Ps 140:3; Dt 32:33; Job 20:16; Ps 58:4; Ro 3:13; Jas 3:8.

POMEGRANATE — Symbol of fruitfulness, joyfulness. Ex 28:34; 39:26; SS 4:3; 6:7; Joel 1:12; Nu 13:23.

POOR — Type of distress, humility. Ps 40:17; 74:19; 86:1; Mt 5:3; 11:5; Mk 12:42-43; Lk 6:20; 2Co 6:10; 8:9.

POTSHERD — Symbol of natural man, of the clay, the earth. A piece of pottery. Isa 45:9; Job 2:8; Ps 22:15; Pr 26:23.

POTTER — Type of God in creative work. Isa 64:8; Jer 18:4-6; La 4:2; Rev 2:27; Isa 29:16.

POUND — Symbol of responsibility, accountability. Weight. Lk 19:13-26.

PRICE

Symbol of value, of worth. 1 Co 6:20; Pr 31:10; Isa 55:1; Mt 13:46; 27:6,9; 1Co 7:23; 1Pe 3:4.

PRIEST

Type of Christ our High Priest, Mediator, Intercessor. Heb 3:1; 2:17; 4:14,15; 6:20; 7:1-26; 8:1-4; 9:7-11; Ps 110.

PRISON

Symbol of bondage, slavery, Sheol or Hades. 1 Pe 3:19; Ps 142:7; Isa 61:1; Rev 20:7; Ps 79:11; 102:20.

PSALTERY

Symbol of praise, worship, rejoicing. A wind instrument. Ps 150:3; 2Sa 6:5; 1Ch 13:8; 15:16-28; Ps 33:2; 71:22; 81:2; 91:3; 144:9.

PURPLE

Symbol of royalty, wealth, prosperity.   Lk 16:19; Jdg 8:26; Rev 18:12-16; SS 3:10; 7:5; Jn 19:1-5; Mk 15:17-20.

QUIVER

Symbol of protection, a covering. Isa 49:2; Jer 5:16; La 3:13; Ps 127:5. Place to hide the arrows, etc. Ge 27:3; Job 29:23.

RAGS

Symbol of poverty. Isa 64:6; Pr 23:21; Jer 38:11,12.

RAIMENT (white)

Symbol of covering. White speaks of purity, righteousness. Rev 3:5,18; 4:4; 19:7-8.

RAIN

Symbol of God's blessing, God's Word and Spirit outpoured. Isa 55:10,11; Dt 32:2; Ps 78:24; Job 29:21,22; Ex 16:4; 1Ki 18:41; Zec 10:1,2; 12:10; Ac 14:27; Hos 6:1-3; Pr 28:3,4.

RAINBOW

Symbol of God's covenant to man, beasts and earth. Ge 9:13; Rev 4:3; 10:1. Seal of the Noahic Covenant.

RAM

Symbol of substitution, sacrifice.   Ge 22. Refer Lamb. Ex 29:15-24.

RAVEN	Symbol of evil, Satan going to and fro. "Darkened, dusky." 1Ki 17:4-6; Ps 147:9; Lk 12:24; Isa 34:11; Pr 30:17; Ge 8:7; Job 1:9.
REAP	Symbol of harvesting, rewarding evil or righteous. Job 4:8; Pr 22:8; Hos 8:7; 10:13; Gal 6:8,9; 1Co 9:11; Mt 13:30-43; Rev 14:14-16; Lev 26:5.
RED	Symbol of suffering, sacrifice or sin. Refer Crimson/Scarlet. Isa 1:18,19; Nah 2:3; Rev 6:4; 12:3; Nu 19:2. Refer Red Heifer.
REED	Symbol of frailty, instability. A stalk or stem. Eze 42:16; 1Ki 14:15; 2Ki 18:21; Isa 36:6; Mt 11:7; 12:20; Lk 7:24; Rev 11:1,2. Measuring or judging. Eze 42:15-20.
REFINE	Symbol of purifying, trial, testing. Isa 48:10; 1:25; Jer 9:7; Zec 13:9; Mal 2:2,3; 1Ch 28:17,18.
REFUGE (Cities)	Symbol of Christ our Refuge, protection, safety for manslaughter. Nu 35; Jos 29 with Ps 46:1; 142:5; Heb 6:18,19; Dt 33:27.
REINS	Symbol of motives of the heart. Ps 26:2; Job 19:27; Ps 7:9; 73:21; Isa 11:5; Jer 17:10; Rev 2:23.
REMNANT	Type of that which is left over, left behind, the faithful few. Rev 12:17; Ezr 9:8; Isa 1:9; 37:31,32; Ro 9:27; 11:5.
REND (rent)	Symbol of grief, anger, schism, division. Eze 13:13; 2Ch 34:27; Joel 2:13; Mt 7:6; Jos 7:6; 1Sa 28:17; Mt 9:16; 26:65; Lk 5:36. "To tear."

REST

Symbol of relaxation, refreshing, cessation from work. Isa 11:10; Ps 132:8,14; Isa 14:3,7; 63:14; Heb 4:9. Rest of God. Mt 11:28-30. Rest in Christ.

RIBBAND
(blue)

Symbol of reminder of God's laws. Nu 15:38 with Jn 14:26.

RICHES

Symbol of possessions, rewards, evil or righteous. Ps 37:16; 39:6; 49:6; Pr 3:16; 8:18; 11:4,28; 13:7; 22:1-4; Ro 2:4; 9:23; Eph 1:7,18; 2:7; 3:8-16; Php 4:19.

RINGS

Symbol of eternity, endlessness. Refer Circle. Also, speaks of authority, power in another's name. Ge 41:42; Est 1:6; Lk 15:22; Ex 25:12-27;

RIVER

Symbol of life-giving flow. Ps 36:8; 46:4; Isa 32:2; 41:18; Jn 7:38,39; Zec 10:11. Rivers of the Holy Spirit.

ROBE

Symbol of covering. Refer Garment/Covering. Isa 61:10; Ex 28:31,34; Rev 6:11; 7:9,13,14.

ROCK
(smitten)

Symbol of Christ crucified, waters of the Spirit flow on the basis of His death. 1 Co 10:4,5; Ex 17:5,6; Jn 4:14; 7:37-39; Rev 22:17.

ROCK
(shelter)

Symbol of hiding in Christ. Ex 33:18-23; Job 24:8; Ps 31:3; 95:1; Isa 2:10; 32:2; Mt 7:24-25; 16:18. Foundation Rock.

ROD

Symbol of rule, chastening, guidance, crushing. Also measuring or judging. Ps 2:9; Rev 2:27; 19:15; 11:1,2; Eze 42:15-20. The rod of iron. Shepherd's rod. Ps 23:4; 89:32. Rod of correction. Pr 13:24; 22:15; 26:3; 29:15.

ROD
(Aaron's)

Symbol of fruitfulness, seal of Aaron's priesthood. Nu 17. Christ's eternal priesthood. Heb 7.

ROOF

Symbol of covering, oversight. Mt 8:8; Ge 19:8; Lk 7:6.

ROOT

Symbol of offspring source, progeny. Root of David. Isa 11:10; Isa 14:29; Rev 5:5; 22:16; Pr 12:3; 1Ti 6:10; Heb 12:15; Job 5:3; Ps 80:9; Isa 53:2.

ROPE

Symbol of bondage, to tie around. Jdg 16:11,12; 1Ki 20:31; Isa 5:18; Ac 27:32.

ROSE
(Sharon)

Symbol of Christ and His church. SS 2:1.

RUBIES

Symbol of preciousness, value, glories. Pr 3:15; Job 28:18; Pr 8:11; 20:15; 31:10.

RUIN

Symbol of man's fall into sin. Pr 26:28; 2Ch 28:23; Eze 18:30; 21:15; 31:13; Isa 23:13; Lk 6:48.

RUN

Symbol of swiftness, movement. Pr 1:6; 2Ch 16:9; Isa 40:31; 59:7; Nah 2:4; Rev 9:9; 1Co 9:24.

SABBATH

Symbol of rest, cessation from work, activity. Intermission. Points ultimately to the kingdom-rest of God and His saints. Ex 16:23-29; Lev 16:31; 23:1-39; 26:34-43; Lk 23:56; Heb 3,4.

SACKCLOTH

Symbol of mourning, sorrow, repentance. Sackcloth and ashes linked. Jer 4:8; Ge 37:34; 2Sa 3:31; Mt 11:21; Lk 10:13; Rev 6:12-17; Jnh 3:5-10; Jer 49:3.

SACRIFICE

Symbol of slaughter, death of another, that which costs something. Animal sacrifice pointed to Christ and His saints especially. Eph 5:2; Lev 1,2,3,4,5,6,7. Heb 10:1-10; Ps 40:6-8; 2Co 5:21; Tit 2:14; 1Ti 2:5; Isa 53:7; Jn 10:18.

SALT

Symbol of incorruptibility, preserve from corruption, covenant, that which endures. Mt 5:13; Lev 2:13; Col 4:6; 2Ch 13:5; Ezr 6:9; 7:22; Mk 9:50; 2Ki 2:20,21. Used also in judgment on people and land. Ge 19:26; Dt 29:23.

SAMSON

Type of Christ as Deliverer, Savior and Judge. "Sunlight, or Brilliant." On negative side, type of backslidden believer. Jdg 13,14; Nu 6; Heb 11:32:40.

SAND

Symbol of multitudinous seed, earthly seed of Abraham, unsaved multitudes. Rev 20:8; Ge 22:17; 32:12; Ro 9:27; Rev 13:1; Ge 13:16; Jos 11:4; Jdg 7:12; Job 29:18; Ps 78:27; 139:18.

SANCTUARY

Symbol of God's dwelling place among men. Ex 25:8,9. The Tabernacle of the Lord. Lev 21:23; 26:31; Jer 51:51; Am 7:9. God's dwelling place in heaven. Ps 20:2; 102:19; 150:1; Heb 8:2; 13:11.

SAPPHIRE

Symbol of beauty, hardness. La 4:7; Ex 24:10; Eze 1:26; 10:1; 28:13; SS 5:14; Isa 54:11.

SCAPEGOAT

Symbol of Christ our Sin-bearer. Refer Goat. Lev 16.

SCARLET

Refer Red/Crimson. Isa 1:18; Rev 17:3,4; 18:12; Mk 15:17; Heb 9:19. Color of sacrifice for sin.

SCEPTER	Symbol of power, rule, kingship, authority. Refer Rod. Ge 49:10; Nu 24:17; Ps 45:6; Isa 14:5; Zec 10:11; Heb 1:8; Amos 1:5; Rev 11:1,2.
SCORPION	Symbol of evil spirits, evil men; that which stings, brings pain. Rev 9:5; Dt 8:15; 1Ki 12:11; 2Ch 10:11; Rev 9:10; Lk 10:19.
SEA	Symbol of restless masses of humanity, the wicked nations. Isa 60;5; 57:20; Jude 13; Eze 26:3,4; Jas 1:6; Hab 2:14; Mic 7:12; Isa 23:4; 11:9.
SEA (of glass)	Symbol of peace, tranquility before God's throne. Rev 4:6; 15:2.
SEAL	Symbol of covenant, mark of God or Satan. Rev 7:2; Eph 4:30; 1:13; 1Ki 21:8; Est 8:8; SS 8:6; Da 12:4; Ro 4:11; 2Ti 2:19; Rev 20:3.
SEAT	Symbol of throne authority. Rev 4:4; Lk 1:52; Rev 2:13; 13:2; 16:10; 11:16; Lk 11:43; 20:46.
SEED	Symbol of fruit or posterity, righteous or wicked offspring. Ge 3:15; 13:15; Jer 31:27; Ge 1:11,12; Job 4:8; Ro 4:16; 1Pe 1:23; 1Co 9:11; Hos 10:12; Gal 6:8; Jn 12:24; 1Co 15:36-38.
SERPENT	Symbol of Satan and evil spirits, wicked men. "To hiss, whisper." "To be sly, cunning." Rev 12:9; 20:2; Ge 3:1-14; 2Co 11:3; Ps 58:4; 91:13; Mt 23:33; Lk 10:19.

SEVEN

Symbol of completeness, perfection, good or evil. Rev 8:2; Ex 23:11,12; 31:15-17; Jude 14; Pr 6:15-17; Mt 12:45; 15:34-37; Ac 6:3; Heb 11:30; Rev 2:1; 3:1; 4:5; 5:1-6; 10:3,4; 12:3.

SEVENTY

Symbol of number prior to increase. The 70 souls into Egypt prior to increase into a nation. Ex 1:5; 15:27; 24:1,9; Ge 46:27; Nu 11:25; Lk 10:1; Da 9:2; 1Ch 21:14; Isa 23:15-17; Mt 18:22.

SEVENTY-FIVE

Symbol of separation, cleansing, purification. Abraham 75 years when separated from Babel. Ge 12:4; 8:5,6; Da 12:5-13.

SHADOW

Symbol of covering, protection. Job 3:5; 8:9; 10:21,22; Ps 17:8; 23:4; 36:7; 57:1; 63:7; 91:1; 102:11-14; Ecc 8:13; Mt 4:16; Lk 1:79. Refer Overshadow.

SHAVE

Symbol of being shorn of strength, power. Refer Hair. Jdg 16:19; Isa 7:20; Job 1:20; 1Co 11:5,6.

SHEEP(fold)

Symbol of God's people, Israel or the Church. Ps 79:13; 95:7; 100:3; 119:176; Isa 53:6,7; Jer 12:3; 23:1; 50:6,17; Mt 9:36; 10:16; Heb 13:20; 1Pe 2:25.

SHEPHERD

Type of Christ and eldership over God's flock, His people. Refer Sheep. Heb 13:20; Jn 10; 1Pe 5:4; Eze 34; Jer 23:1-5.

SHIELD

Symbol of protection. Ps 3:3; Ge 15:1; Dt 33:29; 2Sa 22:3; Ps 28:7; 33:20; 59:11; 84:9-11; 115:9,10; 119:114; Eph 6:16.

SHIP

Symbol of merchandise, business among nations separated by waters. Pr 31:14; 1Ti 1:19; Rev 8:9; Mt 8:24; 14:13; Rev 18:17.

SHOE	Symbol of walk, treading a path. Refer Feet/Walk. Eph 6:15; Dt 33:25; SS 7:1; 1Ki 2:5.
SHOULDER	Symbol of strength, government, support. Isa 9:4; 22:22; Ps 81:10; Job 31:35,36; Mt 23:4; Ge 21:14; Jos 4:5; Isa 46:7; Lk 15:5.
SICKLE (sharp)	Symbol of Word of God, reaping. Joel 3:13; Rev 14:14-19; Mk 4:26:29.
SIEVE	Symbol of sifting, shaking, separation of chaff from wheat, etc. Also testing and proving. Am 9:9; Lk 23:31; Isa 30:28.
SIGHT	Symbol of insight, perception, discernment, understanding. Refer Eyes. Ge 18:3; 2Ch 22:4; 24:2; Job 18:3; 19:15; Ps 9:19; 90:4; Pr 3:4; Mt 11:5; Lk 1:15; Ac 4:19; 8:21;Ro 3:20.
SILVER	Symbol of redemption, price of a soul. Lev 5:15; 27:3-6; Ex 30:11-16; Nu 3:44-51; Ex 36:24; Ps 68:13; 1Co 3:12-15; 1Pe 1:18-20; Mt 27:3-9.
SINGING	Symbol of joy, praise, thanksgiving, worship. Ps 7:17; Ex 15:1; Job 29:13; Ps 9:2; 13:6; 18:49; 21:13; 27:6; Pr 29:6; Isa 12:5; 23:16-19; 16:10; Zec 2:10; Jas 5:13.
SIN OFFERING	Symbol of Christ made sin for us. 1 Pe 2:24; Lev 4,5; 2Co 5:21; Gal 3:13; Eph 5:2; Isa 53:1-10.
SIT	Symbol of rest, finished work, authority. Refer Throne/Seat. Ps 110:1; Heb 10:11-18.
SIX-SIX-SIX	Symbol of Mark of the Beast, Antichrist. Rev 13. Refer "Numbers."

SKINS

Symbol of covering. Ge 3:21; 27:16; Nu 4:1-25.

SLEEP

Symbol of indolence, death, or rest. 1 Th 4:14; Ro 13:11; Lk 9:32; 1Co 15:51; 1Th 5:6-10; Isa 56:10; Eph 5:14; Pr 10:5; Lk 22:45; Ac 13:36.

SLIME-PITS

Symbol of man's sinful works. Ge 14:10.

SMOKE

Symbol of blinding power, good or evil. Ge 19:28; Ex 19:18; SS 3:6; Rev 8:4; 19:3; Ge 15:17; Rev 15:8; Isa 6:4.

SNARE

Symbol of instrument to catch, enslave. Refer Net. Jos 23:13; Jdg 2:3; 1Ki 11:4; Ps 106:36; Hos 9:8; 1Ti 6:9; Ps 18:5; 2Sa 22:6; Ps 91:3.

SNOW

Symbol of whiteness, purity, brilliancy. Ps 51:7; 147:16; Da 7:9; Mk 9:3; Rev 1:14; Mt 28:3; Lam 4:7.

SOAP

Symbol of cleansing, washing. Mal 3:2.

SODOM

Symbol of immorality, vileness. Refer Gomorrah. Idolatry, pride, idleness, prosperity. Eze 16:49,50; Jude 7; Ge 13:10-13; 18:16-28; 19:1-28; Dt 32:32; Isa 3:9; Mt 11:23,24; Rev 11:8.

SONG
(new)

Symbol of joy, praise, freshness in worship. Isa 30:29; Eze 33:32; Ps 96:1; 98:1; Rev 5:9; 14:3.

SOUR

Symbol of false teaching, immaturity. Refer Leaven. Isa 18:5; Jer 31:29,30; Eze 18:2; Hos 4:18.

SOUTH — Symbol of quietness of earth. Opposite to North wind. Job 37:17; Ps 126:4; Lk 12:55; Ac 27:13; 28:13.

SOW — Symbol of scattering seed, righteous or evil seed. Zec 10:9; Job 4:8; Ps 126:5; Hos 2:23; 10:12; Mt 13; Pr 6:14-19; 11:18; 16:23; 22:8; Mk 4:14; 2Co 9:6; Gal 6:7,8.

SPARROW — Symbol of little note, small value. Ps 102:7; Mt 10:29-31; Lk 12:6,7.

SPEAR — Symbol of that which pierces. Jn 19:34; Ps 57:4; Hab 3:11. A lance.

SPIDER — Symbol of wise activity. Job 8:14; Pr 39:28; Isa 59:5.

SPIKENARD — Symbol of fragrance, of Christ to the Father God. SS 1:12; 4:13,14; Mk 14:3; Jn 12:3.

SPOT — Symbol of blemishes, imperfections. 1 Pe 1:19; Lev 13:1-39; Nu 19:2; 28:3; Job 11:15; SS 4:7; Eph 5:27; Heb 9:14; 2Pe 3:14; 2:13; Jude 12.

SPRINKLE — Symbol of cleansing, purifying. Heb 9:13; Ex 29:16-21; Lev 1:5-11; 14:7; 4:17; Nu 8:7; Nu 19; Isa 52:15; 1Pe 1:2.

STAFF — Symbol of strength, guidance. Heb 11:21; Ps 23:4; Isa 9:4; 14:5; Ex 12:11.

STARS — Symbol of Abraham's heavenly seed, spiritual Israel, ministers of the Gospel. Rev 1:20; Nu 24:17; Ge 15:5; Mt 24:29; Rev 12:4; Ge 1:17. Light-bearers. Da 12:3. Falling stars - apostates.

STAR (Morning) — Symbol of Christ arising. Rev 2:28; 22:16; 2Pe 1:19.

STANDING   Symbol of unfinished work.   Uprightness. Holding position. Amos 9:1; Eph 6:13; Zec 6:15; Ac 7:55, 56; Heb 10:11.

STEPS   Symbol of spiritual progress, or digression. Refer Walk. 1 Pe 2:21; Ps 37:23; Ro 4:12; Pr 5:5; Ps 18:36; 37:31; 119:133; 2Co 12:18.

STIFF-NECKED   Symbol of stubbornness, resistance to authority, control.   Dt 31:27; Ps 75:5; Jer 17:23; 2Ch 36:13; Eze 2:4.

STOCKS   Symbol of punishment, correction or torture. Job 13:27; 33:11; Pr 7:22; Jer 20:2-3; 29:26; Ac 16:24.

STONE   Symbol of strength, stability, of Christ and believers. Ps 118:22; 1Sa 25:37; Eze 11:19; 36:26; Ge 49:24; 2Sa 23:3; Isa 8:14; 28:16; Mt 21:4; Eph 2:20; 1 Pe 2:1-7. Refer Corner-Stone/Precious Stones.

STONING   Symbol of death, the stony law. Ex 19:13; 21:28,29; Nu 15:36; 2Ch 10:18; Mt 21:35; Jn 8:5; Ac 7:58,59; Heb 11:37; 12:20.

STORMS   Symbol of distress, trouble, swellings. Job 21:18; 27:21; Ps 55:8; 83:15; 107:29; Isa 28:2; Mk 4:37; Lk 8:23; Ps 148:8.

STORK   Symbol of loneliness. Lev 11:19; Dt 14:18; Ps 104:17; Jer 8:7; Zec 5:9. Flight-bird.

STRAIT   Symbol of that which is beset with difficulties. 1 Sa 13:6; 2Sa 24:14; 2Ki 6:1; Job 36:16; Mt 7:13.

STRAIGHT   Symbol of good direction, not crooked. Jos 6:5,20; 1Sa 6:12; Ps 5:8; Pr 4:25; Isa 40:3,4; 42:16; Mt 3:3; Lk 3:4,5; Jn 1:23; Heb 12:13.

STUBBLE — Symbol of that which is useless, worthless, fire-bound. Isa 5:24; Ex 15:7; Job 21:18; Joel 2:5; Mal 4:1; 1Co 3:2.

STUMBLING-BLOCK — Symbol of obstacle, that trips, a snare. Causes a fall, one to stumble. 1Co 1:23; Ro 11:9; 1Co 8:9; Pr 3:23; 4:12,19; Jer 50:32; Da 11:19; Mal 2:8; 1Pe 2:8.

SUN — Symbol of glory, brightness, light. Linked with moon and stars many times. Ps 84:11; 19:7; Mal 4:2; Mt 17:2; Rev 1:16; 10:1; Ge 37:9; Isa 13:10; SS 6:10; Mt 13:43; Ac 26:13; 1Co 15:41. Resurrection glories of the saints.

SUPPER — Symbol of broken body and shed blood of Jesus. The Lord's Supper. Points to Passover Supper and Marriage Supper of the Lamb. 1 Co 11:23-33; Mt 26:26-28; Mk 14:22-26; Lk 22:14-20; Rev 19:7-9.

SWALLOW — Symbol of a wanderer. Pr 26:2; Ps 84:3; Isa 38:14; Jer 8:7.

SWEAT — Symbol of man's efforts, works, effort of the flesh. Ge 3:19; Eze 44:18; Lk 22:44. Sorrow, result of fall of man.

SWINE — Symbol of uncleanness. Refer Sow/Pig. Ignorance, hypocrisy, unbelievers. Pr 11:22; Mt 7:6; Isa 66:3; 2Pe 2:22.

SWORD (two-edged) — Symbol of the Word of God. Eph 6:17; Heb 4:12; Isa 49:2; Rev 1:16; Dt 32:41; Zec 13:7; Ro 13:4. Also instrument of war, judgment and slaughter of the wicked; God's judgment on the flesh. Lev 26:25; Isa 34:5; Ps 17:13; Eze 21:3-5.

TABERNACLE — Symbol of God's dwelling place among Israel. Refer Sanctuary. Ex 25:8,9; 29:42-44; Nu 1:50-53. Refer <u>Tabernacle of Moses</u> and <u>Tabernacle of David</u> (textbooks).

TABLE (Shewbread) — Symbol of communion, priesthood fellowship, Divine food. Ex 25:23; Jn 6; Ps 23:5; Isa 21:5; 1Co 10:21; Da 11:27; Mal 1:7,12; Eze 41:22; Ps 78:19; Isa 65:11; Lk 16:21.

TABRET — Symbol of praise and worship. A tambourine. Isa 24:8; Ge 31:27; 1Sa 10:5; Job 17:6; Isa 5:12.

TAIL (of scorpions) — Symbol of the end, that which stings, brings death. Rev 9:10,19; Ex 4:4; Dt 28:13; 28:44; Job 40:17; Isa 9:14,15; 19:15; Rev 12:4.

TALEBEARER — Type of a scandal monger, gossiper, stirs up strife with words. Pr 18:8; Lev 19:16; Pr 11:13; 20:19; 26:20-22.

TALENT — Symbol of responsibility and accountability. Mt 25:24-28; 18:24.

TARES — Symbol of false teaching, children of Satan, apostates from the faith. Mt 13:25-40. Degenerates, false grain.

TEARS — Symbol of sorrow, humility, sadness, grief (sometimes joy). Isa 25:8; Job 16:20; Ps 42:3; 126:5; Ecc 4:1; Jer 13:17; Lk 7:38-44; Ac 20:19; Rev 7:17; 21:4.

TEETH — Symbol of sharpness, devouring power. Job 16:9; 4:10; 13:14; 41:14; Ps 3:7; 35:16; 57:4; 58:6; 124:6; Pr 30:14; Isa 41:15; Da 7:5-7; Mt 8:12; Mk 9:18; Ac 7:54; Rev 9:8.

TEMPLE

Symbol of dwelling place of God, of the human body, of Christ Jesus. Refer Palace also. Eph 4:9-16; 2:19-22; Jn 2:20; Rev 11:1,2; Heb 8:1,2; Rev 15:1-5; 11:19.

TEN

Symbol of Law, order, testing and trial. Job 19:3; Ge 31:7; 42:3; Ruth 1:4; Da 1:12-15; 7:24; Mt 25:1; Lk 17:12; Rev 2:10; 12:3; 13:1; Heb 7:2-4; Ex 19,20. The Ten Commandments.

TENT

Symbol of a temporary covering, home for man, as pilgrim and stranger enroute to a city. Outer covering. Ex 26:36; Isa 38:12; 2Co 5:1; Ge 12:8; 13:3,12,18; 18:1-9; Ex 40:1-35.

THIGH

Symbol of strength. Ps 45:3; Da 3:32; Ge 32:25; Jdg 15:8.

THIRTEEN

Symbol of rebellion, backsliding, apostasy, or double portion. Ge 14:4; Jer 1:2; 25:3; 2Ki 15:13,14; 15:17; Eze 1:1. The Twelve apostles plus Jesus = thirteen.

THIRTY

Symbol of age of maturity for ministry. Nu 4:3; Ge 41:46; 2Sa 5:4; Lk 3:23; Mt 26:15.

THISTLE

Symbol of the curse, uselessness. Ge 3:18; 2Ki 14:9; 2Ch 25:18; Hos 10:8.

THORN

Symbol of the curse. Ge 3:18; Pr 26:9; Isa 55:13; Hos 10:8; 2:6; Mt 7:16; Mk 4:7; Lk 8:7,14; Heb 6:8. Thistle or briar.

THREE

Symbol of number of the Godhead: Father, Son and Holy Spirit. Also triune man: spirit, soul and body. 1Th 5:23; Ge 1:1; Mt 28:19-20; Mt 12:40; 27:63; Mk 8:31; Lk 11:5; 13:21; 1Jn 5:7-8; Rev 16:13; 11:9.

THREE-HUNDRED   Symbol of faithful remnant. Jdg 8:4; 15:4.

THRESHING   Symbol of separation, trampling under foot, chastening, judgment. Isa 41:15; Mic 4:13; Hab 3:12; Amos 1:3; Isa 21:10; 41:15; Jer 51:33; 2Ki 13:7.

THROAT   Symbol of swallowing, either good or evil. Ps 5:9; 65:3; 115:7; Pr 23:2; Ro 3:13; Jer 2:25; Mt 18:28; 23:24.

THRONE   Symbol of dignity, rulership, power, kingship. Col 1:16; Ge 41:40; Dt 17:18; 1Ki 16:11; 1:13; Job 36:7; Isa 6:1; 14:13; Ps 9:7; Rev 20:11.

THUNDER   Symbol of God speaking, either in blessing or judgment. 1 Sa 2:10; 7:10; Job 26:14; 40:9; Rev 6:1; 14:2; Ps 18:13; 77:18; 104:7; Jn 12:29; Ps 29:3; Ex 20:18; Rev 11:19; 19:6.

TONGUE   Symbol of language, speech. 1Jn 3:18; Pr 25:15; Hos 7:16; Ps 31:20; Jer 9:3; 23:31; Isa 57:4; Rev 16:10; Ps 34:13; 1Pe 3:10; Jas 1:26; Jas 3:1-8. Used for good or evil, blessing or cursing. Only God can tame the human tongue.

TOOTH   Symbol of biting, devouring. Refer Teeth.

TOPAZ   Symbol of beauty, value, precious gem. Ex 28:17; 39:10; Job 28:19; Eze 28:13; Rev 21:20.

TOWER   Symbol of strength, protection, safety. Ps 61:3; 144:2; Pr 18:10; SS 4:4; Jer 6:27; Mic 4:8; Isa 30:25; Zep 3:6.

TRAP   Symbol of that which catches, ensnares. Refer Snare/Net. Job 18:10; Ps 69:22; Jer 5:26; Ro 11:9.

TREASURE

Symbol of wealth, great values. Ps 135:4; Ex 19:5; Isa 33:6; Col 2:3; 2Co 4:7; Mt 12:35; Lk 6:45; Pr 2:4.

TREES

Symbol of nations, individuals, the church, and Christ Jesus. Isa 55:12; Ps 104:16; 105:33; Ecc 2:5,6; SS 2:3; Isa 7:2; 14:8; 44:14; 61:3; Jer 7:20; Eze 17:24; 31:1-18; Da 4:10-26; Hos 14:6-8; Mt 12:33; 13:31,32.

TRUMPET

Symbol of gathering, the coming of Christ, judgment, blessing. 1 Co 14:8; Ex 19:13-16; Jos 6:5; 1Sa 13:3; 2Sa 2:28; 15:10; 18:16; Heb 12:19; 1Co 15:52; 1Th 4:13-18; Nu 10:1-10.

TURTLEDOVE

Symbol of the Holy Spirit. Refer Dove.

TWELVE

Symbol of Divine government, apostolic government. Mt 14:20; Ex 28:21; Jos 4:20-24; 18:24; Mt 10:1-5; Lk 2:42; Jas 1:1; Rev 7:5-8; Rev 21:12-21; 22:2; Ex 15:27; Mt 19:28; Lev 24:5,6.

TWENTY

Symbol of Divine order. Refer to Two/Ten.

TWENTY-FOUR

Symbol of Priesthood courses and order. Jos 4:2-9,20; 1Ki 19:19; 1Ch 24:3-5; Rev 4:4-10.

TWO

Symbol of witness, testimony, or division, separation. Refer numbers specified and implied in Ge 18,19 and Mt 7. Jn 8:17; Dt 17:6; 19:15; Mt 18:16; Rev 11:2-4; Lk 9:1-2 - for witness. For division - Ex 8:23; 31:18; Ge 1:7,8; Mt 24:40,41.

UNCIRCUMCISED

Symbol of uncleanness, out of covenantal relationship with God and His people. Ge 17; Col 2:13; Isa 52:1; Jer 9:25,26; Eze 28:10; 31:18; Ac 7:51; Eph 2:11.

UNCLEAN — Symbol of that which is impure, abominable, demonic. Mt 10:1; Zec 13:2; Mt 12:43; Mk 1:23-27; 3:11,30; 5:2-8; Lk 6:18; 9:42; 11:24; Ac 5:16; 8:7; 10:14; 2Co 6:17; Eph 5:5; Rev 16:13; 18:2. Often associated with unclean spirits.

UNICORN — Symbol of strength. A wild bull. Nu 23:22; 24:8; Dt 33:17; Job 39:9,10; Ps 92:10; 22:21.

UNLEAVENED — Symbol of purity, sinlessness of Christ. Refer Leaven. Lev 23; Lev 2, Meal offering with no leaven in it. Mt 13:33. Leavened loaves.

UP — Symbol of spiritual direction, upwards to God, progression. Ge 13:1; Isa 2:2-4.

URIM & THUMMIN — Symbol of mind of God. "Lights and Perfections." Nu 27:21; Ex 28:30; Lev 8:8; Dt 33:8; 1Sa 28:6; Ezr 2:63; Ne 7:65.

VAIL (veil) — Symbol of separation from God, that which divides, a screen. Lev 16:15; Ex 26:31-35; Mt 27:51; Heb 10:20; 9:3; 6:19; SS 5:7; Ru 3:15; 2Ch 3:14.

VAPOR — Symbol of transitoriness of life. Jas 4:14; Jer 10:13; 51:16; Job 36:27,33.

VESSEL — Symbol of the human body, instrument to be used for God's glory. Vessels of the temple. 1Th 4:4; 2Ti 2:21; 1Pe 3:7; Ac 9:15; Mt 25:4; Ro 9:22,23; 1Co 4:7; Rev 2:27.

VINE
(dresser)

Symbol of national Israel, of Christ and His Church. Jer 2:21; Eze 15:2; Hos 10:1; Joel 1:7; 2Ki 25:12; Ps 80:15; Isa 5:1; Mt 20:1; 21:28; Mk 12:1; Jn 15:1-16; Ro 15:12; Rev 14:18; Isa 37:31. The Father is the Husbandman; Christ is the True Vine; the Church and believers are the Branches.

VIPER

Symbol of Satan and demonic powers. Hissing. Refer Serpent. Job 20:16; Isa 30:6; 59:5; Ac 28:3; Rev 12:1-9; 20:1-4.

VOICE
(many waters)

Symbol of the majesty, overpowering, words of Christ. Rev 1:15.

VULTURE

Symbol of uncleanness. Refer Bird/Unclean. Symbol of evil spirits most generally. Isa 34:15; Job 28:7; Lev 11:14; Dt 14:13.

WALL

Symbol of protection, separation, security, righteous or evil. Isa 26;1; 60:18; 2:15; 5:5; 49:16; Zec 2:5; 1Sa 25:16; Jer 5:10; 15:20; 39:8; Ps 51:18; 2Ch 8:5; Rev 21,22. Walls of the city of God.

WALK

Symbol of conduct, life-style, behavior. Gal 5:16; Ge 5:22-24; 1Jn 1:6,7; 2Co 5:7; Ro 8:1-4; 2Pe 2:10.

WAR

Symbol of destruction, death, carnage. Final war in heaven, and earth. Rev 12:7,17; 2Co 10:3; Rev 17:14; 19:11,19; Jer 51:20; 1Pe 2:11; 1Ti 1:18; Jas 4:1,2.

WASH

Symbol of cleansing. Isa 1:16; Ge 18:4; Lev 1:9-13; Ps 26:6; 51:2-7; Jer 4:14; Jn 13:5-14; Ac 22:16; Jn 9:7; Rev 1:5,6.

WATCH — Symbol of wakefulness, alertness, on guard. Jer 31:28; 51:12; Isa 29:20; Mt 27;65,66; 24:42; 25:13; Rev 16:15; 1Th 5:6-8; 1Co 16:13; 1Pe 5:8; Rev 3:2; Col 4:2; 2Ti 4:5; 1Pe 1:13.

WATERS — Symbol of the nations of earth; restlessness, under-currents, cross-currents. Rev 17:15; Jer 47:1-3; 46:7,8; Isa 8:7; 17:13.

WATERS (of life) — Symbol of eternal life through Christ. Jn 4:13,14; 7:37-39; Rev 21:6; 22:17. The Holy Spirit flowing. Jn 7:37-39; Mt 3:11-16.

WATERS (bitter) — Symbol of sufferings, bitterness of Calvary. Ex 17:1-6; 15:23-27.

WAVE-SHEAF — Symbol of Christ's resurrection, also the saints. Lev 23:9-14; 1Co 15:20-23; Mt 28:1.

WEIGHT — Symbol of burden, a load, heaviness. 2Co 4:17; Job 28:25; Eze 4:10-16; Heb 12:1; Mt 23:23; 2Co 10:10; Da 5:27; Job 31:6.

WELL — Symbol of refreshment, source of water of life. Isa 12:3; Ex 15:27; Jer 2:13; Jn 1:10; SS 4:15; Pr 10:11; 16:22; 18:4; 5:15; 2Pe 2:17. Twelve wells represent the twelve apostles.

WEST — Symbol of evening, going down of the sun, sunset, day closing. Ps 103:12; 75:6; 107:3; Mt 24:27. (Orientals in speaking of the divisions of the heavens supposes his face is always turned toward the East. East is before him, West is behind him, South to his right, and North to his left (Carl C. Harwood, p. 70).

WHEAT — Symbol of staff of life, bread, of Christ, and of His saints. Mt 3:12; Lk 3:17; Mt 13:25-30; Jn 12:24; Ac 27:38; Ps 81:16; Job 31:40.

WHEEL — Symbol of transport, a circle, speed. Refer Circle. Eze 1; Isa 5:28.

WHIRLWIND — Symbol of hurricane, sweeping power, unable to resist. Isa 17:13; Pr 1:27; 10:25; 2Ki 2:1-11; Job 37:9; Isa 5:28; Hab 3:14; Zec 7:14; Ps 58:9.

WHITE — Symbol of purity, righteousness, holiness. Rev 6:2; 7:9; 19:8,9; 15:16; Ecc 9:8; Isa 1:18; Da 7:9; 12:10; Mt 17:2; 28:3; Ac 1:10;

WHORE(doms) — Symbol of spiritual idolatry, immorality, false doctrines and practices. Hos 1:2; Eze 16:20-36; 23:3-43; Ex 34:15,16; Lev 20:5,6; Dt 31:16; Jdg 2:17; Ps 106:39; Eze 6:9; Rev 17; Pr 7:6-23.

WILDERNESS — Symbol of the world without God, or, a place prepared of God for His own. Ps 78:52; Ge 37:22; Ex 7:16; Job 12:24; 39:5,6; Ac 7:38; SS 3:6; Rev 12; Rev 17.

WILLOW TREE — Symbol of weeping, sorrowful tree. Ps 137:2; Eze 17:5; Lev 23:40; Job 40:22; Isa 15:7; 44:4.

WILD ASS — Symbol of man in natural, unregenerate state, stubborn, self-willed, depraved. "Running wild." Ge 16:12; Ishmael "a wild ass of a man," Lit. Jer 2:24; Job 6:5; 39:5; Ps 104:11; Isa 34:14; Hos 8:9. Refer Ass/Donkey.

WIND — Symbol of powers of God or of Satan, breath of life. Isa 11:15; Nu 11:31; Jn 3:5-8; Eph 4:14; Jude 12; Eze 37:9,10; Jn 20:22. Refer Breath.

WINDOW — Symbol of openness, blessings of heaven. Ge 6:16; 8:6; Jos 2:15-18; SS 2:9; Da 6:10; Mal 3:10.

WINE — Symbol of teaching, blessing, true or false. Fermented wine is false teaching; unfermented wine, true teaching. Ps 60:3; Jer 51:71; Ge 14:18; Ps 104:15; Pr 23:30,31; Hos 3:1; Jn 2:3-10; Rev 6:6; 18:13; Mt 11:19; Jn 15:11; Eph 5:18; Lk 5:37-39.

WINE-SKIN — Symbol of that which holds the wine; structure. Lk 5:37-39; Mt 9:17. The local church (structure) is meant to hold the new wine (teachings of Christ, pure doctrines of the Word). The harlot church is drunk with the wine of fornication, impure doctrines. Rev 17.

WINEPRESS — Symbol of that place where true doctrine is produced by proper study of the Word. If evil wine, then false doctrines pressed out of God's Word. Nu 18:27-30; Dt 15:14; Jdg 6:11; Isa 5:2; Mt 21:33.

WINGS (eagles) — Symbol of supernatural, Divine transport. Rev 12:6,14; Ex 19:4; Ac 8:39. Also Divine defense, protection. Ps 17:8; Dt 32:11; Isa 40:31; Mal 4:2; 2Sa 22:11; Ps 36:7; 61:4; 6:37; 91:4; Mt 23:37; Lk 13:34. Refer Eagle.

WOLF — Symbol of Satan and evil, false ministries, and teachers. Eze 22:27; Jer 5:6; Jn 10:12; Hab 1:8; Zep 3:3; Mt 7:15; 10:16; Lk 10:3; Ac 20:29.

WOMAN	Type of a church, true and virgin, or false and harlotrous. Jer 6:2; Rev 17:1-18; 12:1-19; Pr 12:4; 14:1; 31:10; Isa 24:14; Mic 4:10.
WOOD (shittim)	Symbol of humanity, of Christ, or saints. 2Ti 2:20; Ex 7:19; 26:15; Lev 1:7-17; 14:4-6; 1Co 3:12-15; Rev 9:20; Isa 53:1-3. Christ, the Root out of dry ground, of the stem of Jesse, of David's family tree.
WORM	Symbol of that which is despised; used as instrument of judgment. Mic 7:17 Ps 22:16; Job 25:6; Isa 14:11; Ex 16:20; Job 7:5; 19:26; 21:26; Ac 12:23; Mk 9:44-48.
WORMWOOD	Symbol of bitterness of Satan, Satanic power of death. Dt 29:18; Rev 8:10,11 (Isa 14:12; Rev 12:7-9; Lk 10:18; Heb 2:14); Pr 5:4-6; Jer 9:15; 23:15; La 3:15,19.
YEAR	Symbol of revolution of time, a space of blessing or judgment. Isa 23:15; Ps 65;11; Lk 4:19; Isa 61:2; Job 36:11; Ps 90:4,15; 102:24; Eze 4:5.
YOKE	Symbol of servitude, slavery, or fellowship. Ge 27:40; Lev 26:13; Dt 28:48; Jer 27:8-12; La 1:14; 3:37; Ps 119:71; Ac 15:10; 1Ti 6:1; Gal 5:1; Mt 11:29; 2Co 6:14.
ZION	Symbol of God's rulership, kingship, worship in Mt. Zion. Heb 12:22; Ps 2:6; 48:1,2; 102:16; 110:2; Isa 1:27; 4:4,5; Jer 26:18; Joel 3:17; Rev 14:1-4; Ps 48:1-3.

BIBLIOGRAPHY

RECOMMENDED TEXT BOOKS:

Boyd, James P. Bible Dictionary of Proper Names

Bullinger, Ethelbert W. Figures of Speech Used in the Bible

Bullinger, Ethelbert W. Number in Scripture

Cansdale, G.S. All The Animals of the Bible Lands

Conner, Kevin J. and Malmin, Ken. Interpreting the Scriptures

Conner, Kevin J. The Tabernacle of Moses

Conner, Kevin J. The Tabernacle of David

Conner, Kevin J. The Temple of Solomon

Harwood, Carl C. Handbook of Bible Types and Symbols

Keach, Benjamin. Preaching from the Types and Metaphors of the Bible

Payne, F.C. The Seal of God in Creation

Vallowe, Edward F. Keys to Scripture Numerics

Other Resources Available by Kevin J. Conner

Kevin J. Conner

The Epistle to the Romans
The Church in the New Testament
The Book of Acts
Interpreting the Book of Revelation
The Feasts of Israel
Foundations of Christian Doctrine
The Tabernacle of Moses
The Tabernacle of David
The Temple of Solomon

Kevin J. Conner & Ken Malmin

The Covenants
New Testament Survey
Old Testament Survey
Interpreting the Scriptures

Ask for these resources at your local Christian bookstore.

City Bible Publishing
9200 NE Fremont Portland, Oregon 97220
(503) 253-9020   1-800-777-6057
www.citybiblepublishing.com